THE NFL
GAMEDAY COOKBOOK

D0567564

THE NFL
GAMEDAY COOKBOOK

150 Recipes to Feed the Hungriest Fan
From Preseason to the Super Bowl

by **RAY LAMPE** a.k.a. **DR. BBQ**
foreword by **RICH EISEN**

photographs by **LEIGH BEISCH**

CHRONICLE BOOKS
SAN FRANCISCO

Text copyright © 2008 by the National Football League.
Photographs copyright © 2008 by Leigh Beisch.

Stock photography © 2008 Getty Images
Photographers: Al Messerschmidt: 23; Kevin C. Cox: 31; Matthew Stockman: 35; Jed
Jacobsohn: 41; Jed Jacobsohn: 45; Al Bello: 49; Harry How: 55; Otto Greule Jr: 58;
Jonathan Daniel: 61; Jonathan Daniel: 67; Stephen Dunn: 73; Ezra Shaw: 77; Greg Fiume:
81; Otto Greule Jr: 87; Otto Greule Jr: 91; Jed Jacobsohn: 97; Doug Pensinger: 103; Kevin
C. Cox: 107; Steve Dykes: 111; Ronald Martinez: 131; Doug Pensinger: 137; Otto Greule Jr:
142; Rick Stewart: 145; Jed Jacobsohn: 149; Doug Pensinger: 153; Rick Stewart: 157;
Steve Dykes: 162; Kevin C. Cox: 165; Jamie Squire: 171; Sam Greenwood: 179; Dilip
Vishwanat: 185; Jamie Squire: 191; Al Bello: 197; Jed Jacobsohn: 202; Rick Stewart: 205;
Jim McIsaac: 211; Jed Jacobsohn: 217; Jim McIsaac: 223; Donald Miralle: 229; Kevin C.
Cox: 235; Chris Graythen: 236

All rights reserved. No part of this book may be reproduced in any form without written
permission from the publisher.

Library of Congress Cataloging-in-Publication Data available.

ISBN: 978-0-8118-6395-7

Manufactured in China.

Designed by Public

10 9 8 7 6 5 4 3 2 1

Chronicle Books LLC
680 Second Street
San Francisco, California 94107

www.chroniclebooks.com

CONTENTS

Whether you're a couch potato with a 61-inch high-definition plasma television, or a face painter who likes to freeze in the parking lot five hours before kickoff, or a Grey Poupon eater with a top-notch parking pass and a luxury suite personal seat license, there is and always will be one common denominator that levels the entire NFL fandom playing field. **And that is food. Glorious food.**

It is a time-honored, football Gods-given inalienable right that cuts across every conceivable demographic—the entitlement to stuff yourself silly while watching the game. Think about it.

How many times have you either gone to a game or gone somewhere to watch it with a full stomach only to spend the entire four quarters scarfing down every edible morsel not nailed down? Nachos. Pretzels. Chips of absolutely any size, shape, or variety. Didn't I have lunch about an hour ago? Who cares?!! Peanuts! Hot dogs! Brats. Hamburgers. Wait a minute. I don't want to spoil dinner. But oooh, there's . . . Chicken! Fried, grilled. Mmmm. And wings! Oh yes, you can't forget the wings! Chicken wings! Buffalo wings! Mild. Hot. Spicy hot! Atomic!!

It's almost as if the action of a football being put into play releases some sort of pheromone into the atmosphere that wafts directly into the portion of the neural center that controls a human being's concept of moderation and obliterates it. Nothing allows a person to locate his or her hollow leg more than a big-time National Football League affair. I mean, c'mon. Besides a perfect seat in front of the television, what's the first thing you look for when you hit your friend's house to watch the Super Bowl? The spread, of course. The snacks. The hors d'oeuvres. The appetizers. The main course. The dessert. And, if you're really binging, nuked leftovers hours later.

Even the NFL itself—to use the Emeril vernacular—kicks it up a notch. At the Super Bowl, believe it or not, the toughest ticket to find isn't for the actual Super Bowl. No, the toughest ticket at the big event involves the NFL Tailgate party before the game, usually held in a massive tented complex someplace next to the stadium. Only 10,000 or so fans gain entry to that affair, complete with live entertainment, flowing libations and, most important, lots and lots of free food. And, on that front, the NFL doesn't mess around, tailoring the menu to either the host Super Bowl city or the hometowns of the two Super Bowl partici- pants. For instance, at the tailgate for Super Bowl XLI in Miami, the league served Indianapolis (Colts) tenderloin and Chicago (Bears) brats while the tailgate for Super Bowl XXXVIII in Houston was one huge ribs, chicken and beef barbecue hoe-down.

Yes, every football town has its own flavor (or flava, depending on the city) and, if one is not careful, that can sometimes lead to mass confectionary confusion. Thankfully, there's Dr. BBQ to help us navigate these murky waters.

Indeed, the good doctor, aka Ray Lampe, knows his food stuff. And he's known it for quite some time, ever since he burst onto the scene at the 1994 Illinois state champion- ship and left with the prize for 1st Place Pork. Then came the 1995 Michigan state championship and the 1997 Delaware state championship for 1st Place Chicken, and the 1998 Wilson County Tennessee Grand Champion prize and award for "180" 1st Place Brisket. Dr. BBQ then wrapped up his domination of the '90s with the first of his two titles in a competition known as the "Butt to Butt Championship."

I have no earthly idea what that is, but I think we can all agree it sure does sound impressive. And it certainly helped springboard Dr. BBQ into the new millennium during which he owns scores of trophies for all sorts of deliciousness.

Believe me, the NFL doesn't partner up with anyone just willy-nilly. The league throws its shield and markers around like manhole covers so the fact that the NFL has placed its imprimatur on this here book of fantastic recipes and gameday culinary concepts speaks volumes. Unfortunately, with this book, when we speak our mouths are completely full . . . thanks to Ray and his superb suggestions.

Paging, Dr. BBQ! Paging Dr. BBQ to the kitchen . . .or the backyard . . . or the parking lot . . . STAT!

Bon appetit.

RICH EISEN
NFL network

FOOD,
THE NFL,
AND
ME

I don't think anyone has ever watched an NFL game without eating something. I sure haven't.

To most of us, the food and drink on game day are almost as important as the game itself. It's a wonderful tradition to fire up the grill or brew up a pot of chili in anticipation of a big game. I have done this hundreds of times! From the parking lot to the skybox, from the kitchen to the backyard, cooking and football go hand in hand.

My passion for football and cooking goes all the way back to Morton West High School in Berwyn, Illinois. I played right tackle on the junior varsity football team, and when it came time to pick my classes for sophomore year, I realized that Foods 101 was probably pretty easy and would have a bunch of girls in the class, so I signed up. Well, it wasn't exactly easy, but it wasn't exactly Medieval History either, and it sure was a class full of girls! The real surprise was how much I enjoyed the cooking. I learned how to make blueberry muffins, apple pie, and a crabmeat quiche, all of which my family ate repeatedly.

After high school, my football career ended but cooking stayed with me as a hobby and as a way to eat good food. By my early twenties I'd become a pretty good cook, when my friend Bruce Romanek called and said he'd signed us up for a rib-cooking contest in downtown Chicago. Bruce didn't know how to cook, but he was always up for a party, so I borrowed a grill, bought some ribs, and off we went. We didn't win that day, but it was truly an epiphany for me. The idea of bringing all your stuff out to the event and cooking and serving a great meal to your friends just clicked for me. This fun carried over for me beyond barbecue, and before long I had a suitcase with all the supplies for cooking freshly caught smelt on the shore of Lake Michigan, and I'd converted my briefcase to a mobile Walleye cooking toolbox for trips on the Mississippi River with my old buddy John Petitti. Cooking on the lakeshore or the riverbank is a very close cousin to cooking at the game.

I'm known as "Dr. BBQ" these days because of my history and success on the professional barbecue circuit. At these cook-offs, the mantra is "low and slow" because we cook all night at temperatures well below 300 degrees to produce authentic tender, juicy, smoky barbecue. We all know that this kind of cooking produces ribs, pulled pork, and beef brisket that are wonderful game-day food, but I've got a few other tricks up my sleeve too, and they all work for game-day cooking.

I just love to cook for people, so I use any and all methods that are available to produce good food. Hot grilling may be frowned upon by many barbecue traditionalists, but I say slow smoking and hot grilling are very close cousins and I do both every chance I get. Then there is that big gray area in between the two that I like to call indirect grilling or hot smoking. With all of the wonderful grills and smokers in the stores today, any cook can master all of these methods right in their own backyard.

I love cooking outdoors, but I will take you into the kitchen too. I spent a lot of time there with my late Grandma Julia, better known as Meemee. She was born in France and came through Ellis Island as a young girl. She was a wonderful cook who made pan sauces just like a fancy French cook, but Meemee used oleo and tomato sauce instead of butter and cream because she learned to cook in a coal-mining town in southern Illinois, where life was simple and the luxuries were few. As a young man in my twenties, I realized that Meemee was getting older and if I wanted to continue to eat her wonderful food, it would be wise to learn how to cook it. As you can probably guess, she didn't measure much when she cooked. She didn't need to; she already knew how much to put in. So I followed her around and measured the ingredients before she put them in the pot. I'm sure this seemed ridiculous to her, but it was a great success for me. You'll find some of her recipes in this book and you'll enjoy her influence in most of my cooking.

Much of my food is also influenced by the places where I get to cook. I like to refer to myself as a parking-lot chef. I get to travel a lot and I usually cook something while I'm there. But since I'm a barbecue man, they don't put me in the kitchen. I get to cook along the riverbank or on a street corner or in a park or in the loading dock. It's always an adventure and I love it. You meet some very interesting people when you're cooking on the street corner! And every one of them has a food story to tell. It's either about the marinade they made last night or the barbecue sauce they've been making for forty years or the best ribs they ever ate at a little place in a little town in anywhere, U.S.A.

Of course the ongoing conversation about who makes the best ribs gets every-one's attention. Aren't we all really on a life's mission to eat the perfect barbe-cued rib? I have a hard time driving by a funky little barbecue joint because if I don't stop, I might just be driving by the best place ever, and how will I make my life's decision about the best ribs ever knowing that I skipped that place? Sound familiar? (For the record, the best ribs I've ever eaten came from Neely's Interstate Barbecue in Memphis, and I ate them driving down I-57. Hey—it's barbecue.) With all barbecue restaurants, your experience may vary because ribs don't hold up very well and most of the old barbecue joints don't have fancy holding equipment. When it's done, it's done, and if you're lucky enough to be there at the perfect time like I was that day, it's nirvana. My second-best rib experience was a very similar story and the ribs were eaten while driving down I-10. Those ribs came from the original Dreamland BBQ in Tuscaloosa, Alabama, and they were fabulous.

I've also spent a considerable amount of time cooking outside of an NFL stadium. I grew up in Chicago and one of my earliest NFL memories was a Bears game at Wrigley Field with my father. We didn't tailgate that day—my dad wasn't much of a cook—but there were a couple of decades later in my life when I was a regular in the parking lot outside Soldier Field on Sunday mornings when the Bears were at home. A group of a dozen friends would take turns bringing the food and drink for the tailgate parties. We'd meet at Otto's Bar, light the grill, and drive the twenty minutes down the highway with it lit in the back of a pickup truck. I no longer recommend this technique, but it worked for us. As I learned to cook,

I also became the guy in charge of the Super Bowl party food for my friends. I think I prepared a dozen different courses on some of those days.

As I look back from the age of fifty, I realize that NFL football and cooking great food for my family and friends have been constant and important things in my life. The first autograph I ever collected was from football great Gale Sayers, and the first book I remember reading by choice was *Farewell to Football* by Jerry Kramer. In the spirit of Al Bundy, I even have a couple of trophies for playing football in my younger days. (Make that MUCH younger days.) As I look at the bookshelf in my office now, I see books by football and food authors such as Mike Ditka, George Halas, Julia Child, and Rick Bayless. There are old copies of sports and food magazines too. The collection includes *Gourmet, Food and Wine, Fiery Foods*, and *Sports Illustrated.* On another shelf is a picture of me with Nancy Faust—the longtime organist at White Sox games—and a hat that promotes "Pork" signed by Frank Kimmel, a racecar driver. Last but not least, this whole second career as a chef and food writer that I'm enjoying has been based on my background competing in big-money barbecue contests, which many consider sporting events. I feel like a very lucky man, because I've spent most of my life preparing to write this book without even knowing it.

So now you know a little bit about me and my love of NFL football and food. The two subjects just go together beautifully. In this book I'll offer up a whole chapter on the things you'll need to make some of my fun and exciting recipes at home or at the game. I'll suggest great ways to keep things hot and fresh for the ride to the game or just so you can have them ready for halftime at home. We'll fry some things and grill some things and even use a great outdoor wok for a big stir-fry. The other chapters will focus on different food groupings, from appetizers to desserts and even a few drinks for your party.

Most of the dishes are designed to be elegant enough to serve at home, yet sturdy enough to travel to the game, but they'll all have one thing in common: It's all real food that people like to eat. There are no trendy little stacks of food that you can't identify in my world. Some of the recipes here will need to be finished at the last minute on the grill and others will be best cooked ahead. My suggestion is to pick one or two from each category to create the game-day menu that you like the best. For some game-day parties, a few dishes will do, but if you're like me, that big Super Bowl party will have you cooking half the book!

I hope you enjoy my recipes as much as I've enjoyed creating them. I'll be proud to have you prepare them for your menu. Please always remember that it's your menu. These recipes aren't set in stone. If you like a little more garlic or a little less hot pepper, go right ahead and make it your way. That's the fun of cooking. It's an art and your creativity should be part of it. And if you want to serve a salsa with the baked ziti and the fried rice, go ahead. It's your party and you can have it any way you want! Just call it NFL game-day fusion cooking.

Ray

The Equipment Room

Just like your favorite team needs all the right equipment on game day, so does the cook. Most of us don't have our own equipment manager, though, so we need to get everything in order ourselves. But as any gadget-loving guy will tell you, this can be half the fun. The needs are going to be different depending on where your game-day feast will be held. If it's at your house, it's pretty easy, and if it's taking a dish or two to a friend's house, it won't be too hard either. But if it's at the game or some other exotic location, you're going to have to be organized and bring all the right stuff. After all, nobody wants to eat cold turkey while sitting on the ground. Your equipment needs are also going to vary widely depending on how many guests you'll be feeding and how many other cooks will be bringing food. If it's six friends at your house, you can get ambitious and buck up for the lobsters and use the real wine glasses; if it's forty guests in a parking lot, you'll be better off with a big pot of chili and cans of beer. I've done big and small and it's all fun, so jump right in and get cooking. I'm going to talk about some fancy stuff here, but not to worry. A good parking lot chef can always improvise. That's what makes it fun.

GRILLING

Grilling is probably the number one cooking method on game day. Almost everyone has a grill and we all love grilled food, so it's a natural. I like to use my grill in many different ways for my meals. You'll often see a pot or a pan simmering next to my grilled burgers or brats. Just be sure to use a disposable pan or something that won't be needed in the kitchen anymore, because it will get discolored and look kind of rough. I like to think of it as patina.

Charcoal Grills

I always prefer charcoal grilling because the food just plain tastes better. It's no secret that interest in grilling is growing by the day, and as people get more into it they are appreciating the taste of charcoal cooking, so these grills are getting very popular again.

It may be a little more hassle than a gas grill, but if you get all the right equipment in place it's easily worth the trouble. My favorite charcoal grill is the Big Green Egg. It's made of ceramic and holds the heat beautifully for grilling or smoking. The large one is a bit heavy for tailgating at 150 pounds, but I take mine with me all the time. If you're not that ambitious, maybe a lightweight metal kettle grill is for you. These are wildly popular and they work very well. There is also a newfound popularity for large, square charcoal grills these days. They are big and macho and can cook a lot of food. For home use these are the best choices for game-day cooking. If you drive a pickup truck or a van, you'll be good with any of these for traveling to the game. If you'll be using the family SUV or your Mustang for carrying your equipment to the game, you're gonna need to downsize on the grill. The kettle grill companies all make smaller versions and they work well. There's a small Big Green Egg too, and you can always just get a basic cheapy grill with three legs and a grate. You'll be limited as to what you can cook on the cheapy without a cover, but you'll still have that great charcoal taste.

Speaking of charcoal, there are a few kinds and you'll have to make a choice. There are two main types of charcoal. There are the briquettes that we are all familiar with, which are shaped like little pillows and were invented by Henry Ford—yes, the car guy. You'll probably find a couple brands available locally, and while all of them have something added besides the charred wood, they're all pretty reliable. Then there is lump charcoal, which is used all over the world and is becoming very popular throughout the United States. Lump charcoal is made of charred wood. That's it. No additives. There are many different brands. The primary differences in brands are the type of wood they start with and the process they use to carbonize it. For everything you ever wanted to know about lump charcoal visit www.lump-charcoal.com. (Don't forget the hyphen.) It's an amazing resource, but this guy clearly has way too much time on his hands.

The short answer to the question of what to use is that I prefer lump charcoal because it makes the food taste better, but I've cooked a lot of good food with briquettes too. One type of charcoal I will never use is that self-lighting stuff. The premise is that it's soaked in lighter fluid, so all you do is take a match to it and it'll light itself. This is not a good thing. I'll use lighter fluid if nothing else is available, but I try to use as little of it as possible and I make sure to let it all burn off before the food goes on. With the presoaked stuff, that's just not possible, so the food is bound to have some taste of the lighter fluid.

The best way to light briquettes is with a charcoal chimney. These have become very popular and are available every-where. You use a couple sheets of newspaper to get a big mug of coals going, and then you dump them in the grill to mix with some unlit coals that will get lit quickly. A charcoal chimney is a quick and efficient way to start a charcoal fire, and it can be used with lump charcoal too, but I don't feel it's the best choice for lump. Lump charcoal is much lighter and less dense than briquettes and it lights very easily. I like to use a few small pieces of a paraffin/sawdust–based fire starter. You'll find this type of starter either in little squares designed for grill lighting or in bigger sticks intended for starting the campfire or fire-place. Either will work; just cut off three or four small pieces, push them down into the pile of lump, and light them. In about 10 minutes, or as soon as the paraffin has burned off, you can start cooking. This is not your father's charcoal cooking!

Gas Grills

Gas grills are the most popular outdoor cooking tools and it's easy to see why. All you do is turn the knob and push the button, and after a brief warm-up you're ready to cook. For game-day cooking at home, you'll be able to fit a lot of food on the grill, and many even have a side burner for heating the sauce or cooking a side dish. Others go way beyond the side burner and offer a deep fryer, griddle, smoker box, and rotisserie. They may come with big cabinets that have warming drawers and cooling drawers and even a place for the garbage. These are truly the weapons of choice for any guy who wants to be the king of his backyard.

I'm more about the cooking than I am about the gadgets, though, and there are a few helpful options that you should consider when choosing a gas grill. They all have multiple burners, which are great for using different heat levels in different areas of the grill. Many have three, four, or even more burners in a left-to-right configuration. Others have three burners that run across the cooker and are con-figured front-to-back. I prefer the side-to-side setup because I won't have to reach over one zone to get the food to another, which could mean putting my hand in a hot spot and causing one of my dishes to drip on another as I retrieve it. In the side-to-side arrangement everything has its own zone and each zone can be easily reached.

Last, but certainly not least, are the infrared burners. These are similar to what the local steakhouse is using when they brag about cooking at 1,000 degrees or more. They do one thing very well and that is to get really hot. If you're cooking steaks, chops, or burgers, these are great; if you're cooking something a little more delicate or trying to cook a few different things that require lower temps, the infrared burners might not be the best choice for you.

A great option that has come out with many of the larger gas grills is a combination of burners. This is a really good idea since you can have an infrared burner on the left for blazing your steak, a standard gas burner in the center for your chicken, a back burner for your rotisserie, and a side burner for your beans. The combinations are endless and only your budget can control what is possible. Once again, these are big homebound units and, except for the more ambitious game-day cooks, that is where they should stay.

Of course we've all seen (or been) the guy with his big gas grill in the back of his pickup truck on a Sunday morning, but for most of us that's not an option. The good news is there are many great portable gas grills available that will save you that hassle and cook some good food at the game. My favorite is the Freestyle Portable Grill made by Napoleon. It has an optional bracket that goes right in the hitch receiver on the back of my van so it rides along right there at the perfect cooking height. It stays right there to cook on and is hassle-free the whole day. I have the infra-red version because I mainly use it for quick grilling jobs, but they have a model with a traditional burner too. The collapsible gas grills that have the cast-iron grates are very nice too. They fold up like a suitcase and fit anywhere for travel, but at the game they open up to a sizeable grilling surface and they cook very evenly. There are also the old-school portable grills that look kind of like a toolbox and they will get the job done as well. They're just not as flashy and they don't get as hot or cook as evenly.

Pellet, Electric, and Newspaper-Fired Grills

I'm not sure whatever happened to that newspaper-fueled grill that Dick Butkus was promoting on the beach, but I'm sure sorry I didn't buy one. They looked to be having a lot of fun and Butkus sure could cook well on it. If I hear any more about it I'll let you know. The news about pellet-fired grills and electric grills is much better. These types of grills are alive and kicking. The pellet grills burn wood that is formed into little rabbit food–shaped pellets that are automatically fed into a firepot for burning. They're often thermostatically controlled and the temps will be very even. Unfortunately they don't really get hot enough for a serious sear on steaks or chops, but for slower grilling they are excellent, and the 100 percent wood fueling creates a great taste. Mainly for this reason, cooking with wood pellets has become very popular on the barbecue contest circuit. Not so much for electric grills, which aren't the best at much of anything except pleasing the condo board. Many places don't allow open fires on their balconies or patios because of the danger of fire, so an electric grill is the only option. I guess it's better than nothing, but they're not recommended by me. I'd move.

SMOKERS

A smoker has become a part of many cooks' arsenals these days and I think that's good news. People love smoked food and they're learning how to cook it at home. I'm not talking about cold smoking, which is done at temperatures below 100 degrees and doesn't actually cook the food; I'm talking about hot smoking, which is also known as "real barbecue." I have great love for this type of cooking as I've spent literally hundreds of weekends in parks and parking lots competing on the barbecue competition trail. At these contests, we cook big briskets and pork shoulders for ten to fifteen hours, slowly melting them overnight into tender and smoky barbecue. This can only be done at low temps, usually between 225 and 250 degrees.

Most grills can be adapted to do a reasonable job of this, even the gassers, but if you like this kind of food you'll find it much better to buy the right kind of equipment. You can call Roger Davidson at Horizon Smokers in Oklahoma and order up a big log-burning steel pit on a trailer with the firebox set off to the side and a fancy prep table built in and shiny mag wheels. This will cost you about the same as a car and it will impress everyone who sees it. It'll last your whole life. It'll cook great barbecue too, so if that all sounds good to you, you're all set. If your budget is a little tighter and something a little less flashy is your thing, you might consider one of the many charcoal-burning box-shaped smokers that many of the cook-off guys are using. I've always thought that cooking above the fire made more sense than the offset configuration, so I like these. Check out Backwoods, Spicewine, and Jedmaster to see some of them.

Like I said, any grill can do a reasonable job, but the Big Green Egg truly is a great grill *and* a great smoker. Be sure to consider one for your arsenal as well as the very popular bullet-shaped water smokers. These will typically be an R2-D2–looking thing with the fire in the bottom, a pan of water above the fire to deflect the heat, and two racks for the food above. They work very well and many a big barbecue cook-off has been won using them. They're also pretty affordable, with the upscale Weber version coming in around $300 and the el cheapo versions at well under $100. The pellet cookers step up very well in the smoker department. They may not be good at searing but they are great at long, unattended, slow smoking. Look for the Traeger brand or the big and beautiful Fast Eddy pellet cookers made by Cookshack. Speaking of Cookshack, they are also the leader in the electric smoker industry, and much like the pellet cookers, electric smokers do very well at slow smoking. You just load it up and forget about it until the food is ready.

STOVES

Game-day man cannot live on grilled and smoked foods alone, so we're gonna need a stove. I'll skip over home stoves. You probably already have one of those anyway. For cooking at the game there are many choices and you should take into consideration what it is that you like to cook. If you think that one burner for occasionally heating small things will do it for you, then consider a single-burner butane stove. They're very convenient—even coming in a carrying case—and the whole thing is compact and easily stashed for the ride. You'll have to be sure to keep some of the little butane bottles around, but they're pretty easy to find. Look for the stove and the butane in camping supply stores. When you're in the camping department, look around and you'll see the bigger portable stoves too. If you like to cook a big breakfast for your guests or warm a big pot of soup or chili, you might consider a camping stove. These come in many shapes and sizes and use many different fuels. I like the big three-burner model that runs on propane bottles. It's not much bigger than the two-burner and the propane is pretty much hassle-free as long as you remember to bring a spare bottle. One downside to the traditional camping stove is that it will take up some valuable table space. Look for the new stoves that have fold-up legs built right in to solve this problem. Some are even stove-grill hybrids that are very useful on game day and may even come with built-in wheels.

OTHER GREAT COOKING DEVICES

Grills, smokers, and stoves are the traditional cooking devices that we all know and love, but there are some other exciting tools that should also be considered. First is a close cousin to the stove and an amazing tool. Coleman makes a camping oven that fits a full 9-x-13–inch pan or a similar-sized cookie sheet and is fueled by a one-pound propane bottle. It's like a large toaster oven that you can use anywhere. They also have a slow cooker and a skillet that work the same way. Coleman is also the company that makes the Hot Water–On-Demand portable water heater that runs on a one-pound propane cylinder. Almost every barbecue competitor I know has one of those. This is all great stuff for cooking in the parking lot.

Next is the turkey fryer. Many of us have one that we break out for Thanksgiving but forget about the rest of the year. Frying a turkey on game day is always a great idea. It's exciting to do, it feeds a lot of guests, and turkey is pretty cheap. I always buy a few extra turkeys when they're on sale during the holidays and then I can eat turkey all year long. That turkey fryer is good for a lot of other things too. I went to a Bucfanz.com tailgate party last year in Tampa and a guy was frying fish and French fries in his for the guests to enjoy before the game. I've fried shrimp and chicken and Twinkies and Oreos in mine and it was all great. (Just dip the Twinkies and Oreos in a simple batter and fry them fast.) You can also use it to steam and boil stuff. Corn comes to mind and so do lobsters. Just keep in mind that frying can be dangerous if you're not careful. Be sure to read the manufacturer's instructions before you start and follow all of their safety recommendations.

I recently came across another tool that is similar to the propane turkey fryer, but instead of the pot it includes a 22-inch wok. This thing is called the Big Kahuna Wok Kit and it's made by Eastman Outdoors. I got it to test out the fried rice and stir-fry recipes for this book and it was a real pleasure to use. I've never been satisfied using a wok at home because it just doesn't get hot enough. Well, that problem is over with this baby. When I put the rice in, it didn't even slow down! The rice actually fried instead of steaming. It's also a big enough wok to cook for a crowd, and the legs on the burner adjust up and down for a comfortable cooking height and compact travel. I'll be using my wok kit a lot.

COOLERS, WARMERS, CONTAINERS, AND PANS

There is an amazing array of different cooler styles available these days. I like the ones with wheels because they are easy to move around. I like the stainless ones because they look nice and are easy to keep clean, and I really like the ones that come with stands so I don't have to bend over to get a beverage. The real lessons to learn about coolers are to use one that's big enough to fit some ice if you're keeping things cold and to always keep the raw meat in a separate cooler from the stuff that won't be cooked and the drinks. It's a serious food-safety issue to have the raw meat in with the cold drinks, and if you were a caterer the health inspector would shut you down if he saw that. Coolers can be used to hold hot food as well. Just skip the ice and put a couple hot pans of food or a bunch of individually wrapped ribs, fresh from the cooker, in a cooler and close the lid. No peeking, keep it shut, and the food will stay hot for hours. You may want to line the bottom of the cooler first with newspaper or an old towel to keep it from warping.

The professional version of this is called a Cambro, which really isn't correct because that's actually the name of the company that makes most of them. The real name is Insulated Front-Loading Food Pan Carrier, and they match perfectly with restaurant-sized pans. The pans slide in and stay in place while staying hot. There is a smaller version that holds one pan and opens on top too. It's called an Insulated Top-Loading Food Pan Carrier. It's a bit of an investment, but a Cambro and some restaurant pans with lids make carrying hot food to a friend's house or the game a simple task. Most restaurant-supply companies have a retail store and will sell to the public, so check them out.

About those restaurant pans, here's the deal: There are two basic sizes of rectangular pans in the restaurant business. One is the hotel pan, and one is the sheet pan. The hotel pan, a.k.a. steam table pan, is 12 x 20 inches and comes in a variety of depths, such as 2-inch, 4-inch, and 6-inch. Sheet pans are 18 x 26 inches, and are typically about an inch deep. Both are universally accepted, and all the racks, steam tables, chafing dishes, lids, and such are interchangeable. There are also cut-down versions that are called half and quarter pans, and hotel pans even go down to sixth and ninth pans. So, in a standard-size restaurant steam table you could have one half pan with one item in it, and two quarter pans with some other items all nestled in one hotel pan–sized space. If you pay attention at your next visit to the mega buffet, you'll see many of these pans in use. I think you'll find the half-size sheet pans and hotel pans to be very useful in a home kitchen. The same sizing is used for square plastic containers to be used for dry storage and refrigerated items. Look for them at the restaurant-supply store or at the warehouse club.

These pans aren't really meant for cooking on the stove or grill, although the disposable ones are great for the grill. You will find half-size and full-size disposable aluminum pans at the warehouse club. I use these all the time around the grill and on it, too. They are considerably cheaper than the turkey roaster–type pans you'll see at the grocery store, and made better too. If you decide to buy a Cambro, be sure to think about the size that you want. Probably a hotel-pan size would be best. That is also the size of a typical chafing dish, so if you use those you can transfer the pan directly from the Cambro to the chafing dish with no mess and no fuss. Just fire up a couple of Sternos and the food will stay hot for hours of service.

Another popular choice for cooking on the grill is a cast-iron Dutch oven. I find that the one I use on the grill is best left to only that task because it gets a little greasy for the kitchen. I also have a couple of saucepans reserved for the grill and they get used pretty often. Indoors, I typically use a 6-quart nonstick heavy-duty Dutch oven. The indoor cast-iron Dutch oven would work too, but I find nonstick to be my friend when making stews, soups, chilis, and sticky sauces. My skillets in the kitchen are 10-inch and 12-inch nonstick. My saucepans are a 2-quart and a 4-quart. My big stockpot is a 20-quart stainless-steel pot with a heavy bottom.

ODDS AND ENDS

I don't buy expensive fancy knives for myself. If you went into some of the professional kitchens that I've visited and saw how bad the knife situation was, you'd be amazed. We all have this vision of a restaurant kitchen keeping the knives razor-sharp and in a special holder, when the reality is many of them keep the knives in a big pan and they aren't very sharp. I like to keep my knives reasonably sharp, but in the real world of cooking it's not always possible. My favorite knives around the kitchen are a 7-inch boning knife and a 10-inch chef's knife. For chopping barbecue, I use a 14-inch scimitar that looks like a pirate should be holding it. It works well and keeps people from getting too close.

//// For my instant-read thermometer—which I consider invaluable for testing the doneness of meats—I use a Thermapen made by Thermoworks. It's a little pricey but it's simply the best.

//// For cleaning my grill grid and generally poking stuff, I use a Billy Bar. It's a simple but great tool made of cast iron with a wooden handle. It has a "Y"-shaped end that fits perfectly to the shape of the grill grates for scraping off the crud.

//// I always have a pair of heavy welder's gloves around and a pair of those silicone mittens to protect my hands when I'm handling hot grates or accessories.

//// I always have a box of latex gloves around too, although I'm not a real doctor. I use them to keep my hands clean when I'm handling dirty grates and charcoal but also to keep things clean when I'm handling the food. Always use a clean pair to handle the food.

//// I keep a pop-up shelter in my van all the time. Shade is a good thing on a hot day, and you can get one with your team's logo on it at NFL.com.

//// Chairs with your team's logo are a good addition too, and since the cook won't have a chance to sit down much I like to bring a bar stool along for a quick rest here and there.

//// Clean-up and cross-contamination are serious issues. Once you use a plate for raw meat you can't use it for cooked meat or anything else that people will eat until it's thoroughly washed with hot soapy water. WIPING IT OFF IS NOT OK. The same goes for knives and cutting boards and everything else you use for raw meat or fish. If you won't be able to clean up with hot soapy water and a good rinse, just bring two sets of what you'll need. Use one for the raw food and one for the cooked food. Don't even keep the contaminated raw food plate around. It's nasty to have hanging around, and you might use it by accident. Take it in the house or put it away with the dirty dishes as soon as you are done with it. WIPING IT OFF IS NOT OK!

Some doneness temps for grilled food are as follows:

MEAT	DONENESS	INTERNAL TEMPERATURE
Steak	rare	120
Steak	medium	140
Ground beef	cooked medium and safely done	155
Pork	done safely	137
Pork	done just a little pink	145
Pork	done per the USDA	160
Pork	done the way your grandma did it	180
Poultry, white meat	done safely	160
Poultry, dark meat	done safely	180

MEAT, SPICES, AND SAUCE

Most of the time, when I cook for someone, they are surprised at how humble my meat choices are. I guess they expect me to have some exotic source for beef that they haven't heard of and some farmer in Iowa raising some special hogs for me, or a cage of fresh chickens in the back of my van. That's not the kind of cook that I am. The true roots of barbecue are those of the poor and the slaves, who took the lesser cuts and made wonderful dishes out of them. My life is much more fortunate than that, but that's just how I think about cooking. I take a lot of pride in my ability to cook the stuff that's in the butcher case at the grocery store. I figure that's what most of you are buying, so it's best if I start the recipe that way. Now don't get me wrong—I buy first-quality pork, but see no reason to buy it at the fancy butcher shop. Odds are it's the same pork. You just get it wrapped up while you wait instead of grabbing it out of the case and you get to pay more. Same with beef. Be sure you're buying USDA Choice-graded beef and you'll be getting pretty good stuff no matter where you buy it. If you want to spring for some USDA Prime-graded steaks once in a while, go for it, but day to day the stuff at the grocery store is fine. When it comes to chicken, I try to buy fresh, all-natural when I can. A lot of chicken now is "enhanced" with a salt solution to make it stay juicy, last longer, and taste better. It's not really a bad thing—matter of fact, some of it tastes pretty good—but I try to avoid it if I can. I'd rather season the chicken myself. Occasionally you'll see pork and beef that is also "enhanced." The pork can be OK, but try to avoid the beef at all costs. It's just not a good thing for beef.

When I create my recipes I try to also use the dry ingredients that I think you're using, so I buy most of my spices at the warehouse club or the grocery store. Chili powder is the one exception. The stuff in the stores just isn't very good, so I order that online from a company in Fort Worth called Pendery's. They're also a great source for things like ancho chile powder and ground chipotles, which most grocery stores don't carry. While you're ordering, you might want to try the granulated onion and garlic from them as well. It's great stuff for dry rubs. I also order small plastic spice shakers from them. If you make your own rubs you'll find these to be very handy.

I've included three homemade barbecue rub recipes and three homemade barbecue sauce recipes here, and I hope you'll try them, but I must tell you that some of my friends on the contest circuit are producing some great microbrew-type rubs and sauces that I also use regularly. A couple of my favorite store-bought rubs are from Head Country, Smoking Guns, and Dizzy Pig. As for sauces, I'd suggest trying Texas Rib Rangers, Head Country, and Blues Hog. A good online source for all of these rubs and sauces is Hawgeyesbbq.com in Ankeny, Iowa. On a much less exotic note, I often call for seasoning salt in my recipes. I use Lawry's Seasoned Salt a lot in my kitchen and I have for years.

When I call for your favorite barbecue rub or sauce in my recipes, I'd like you to consider the recipes below, the store-bought suggestions above, or your favorite that I don't even know about yet.

½ cup seasoned salt, such as Lawry's

¼ cup packed brown sugar

¼ cup turbinado sugar (Sugar in the Raw)

1 tablespoon granulated garlic

1 tablespoon granulated onion

1 tablespoon paprika

1 teaspoon dry mustard

1 teaspoon celery seed

1 teaspoon black pepper

½ teaspoon cayenne

½ teaspoon ground nutmeg

Extra Point Barbecue Rub

This rub is very middle-of-the-road and works well on many things.

Combine the ingredients in a small bowl and mix well. Store in an airtight container for up to 1 month.

MAKES ABOUT 1¼ CUPS

Touchdown Barbecue Rub

This rub is very middle-of-the-road and works well on many things.

½ cup salt

½ cup turbinado sugar
(Sugar in the Raw)

¼ cup granulated brown sugar

¼ cup good-quality chili powder

2 tablespoons lemon pepper

2 tablespoons granulated garlic

1 tablespoon granulated onion

1 tablespoon ground cumin

2 teaspoons dried thyme leaves

1 teaspoon cayenne

Combine the ingredients in a small bowl and mix well. Store in an airtight container for up to 1 month.

MAKES ABOUT 1½ CUPS

End Zone Barbecue Rub

This rub is a little on the salty side, with a unique taste from the coffee.

½ cup salt

½ cup packed brown sugar

2 tablespoons good-quality chili powder

1 tablespoon ground coffee

1 tablespoon lemon pepper

Combine the ingredients in a small bowl and mix well. Store in an airtight container for up to 1 month.

MAKES ABOUT 1¼ CUPS

Honey Bears Barbecue Sauce

This is a sweet and tasty sauce named in honor of some old friends.

2 cups tomato sauce

1 cup honey

¼ cup of the juice from a jar of maraschino cherries

2 tablespoons granulated onion

1 tablespoon granulated garlic

1 tablespoon black pepper

1 tablespoon white vinegar

1 tablespoon soy sauce

1 tablespoon Worcestershire sauce

½ teaspoon salt

Add all the ingredients to a medium saucepan over medium heat. Mix constantly and heat for 5 minutes or until well blended. Store in an airtight container in the refrigerator for up to 2 weeks.

MAKES ABOUT 3 CUPS

1 cup V-8 vegetable juice

1 cup prepared chili sauce

½ cup corn syrup with
brown sugar

¼ cup yellow mustard

2 tablespoons brown sugar

1 teaspoon granulated garlic

1 teaspoon granulated onion

½ teaspoon cayenne

½ teaspoon celery seed

¼ teaspoon salt

Midfield Barbecue Sauce

This sauce is a little bit tangy and good on everything.

Add all the ingredients to a medium saucepan over medium heat. Mix constantly and heat for 5 minutes or until well blended. Store in an airtight container in the refrigerator for up to 2 weeks.

MAKES ABOUT 3 CUPS

---

2 tablespoons vegetable oil

½ cup minced onion

1 clove garlic, minced

1 jalapeño, minced (seeds optional)

1 serrano chile, minced (seeds optional)

2 cups ketchup

¼ cup yellow mustard

¼ cup molasses

¼ cup Frank's or other vinegar-based
hot sauce (optional)

2 tablespoons good-quality chili powder

1 tablespoon Worcestershire sauce

1 tablespoon soy sauce

Sudden Death Barbecue Sauce

This one is hot if you leave the seeds in the chiles and use the hot sauce. If you use something hotter than Frank's, you're on your own.

In a small saucepan over medium heat, warm the oil. Add the onion, garlic, and chiles and cook, stirring occasionally, until everything is soft, about 4 minutes. Add the ketchup, mustard, molasses, hot sauce (if using), chili powder, Worcestershire, and soy sauce. Bring to a simmer and cook for 15 minutes, stirring often. Store in an airtight container in the refrigerator for up to 2 weeks.

MAKES ABOUT 3 CUPS

Arizona Cardinals

1920–1943, 1945–1959 Chicago Cardinals, 1944 Card-Pitt, 1960–1987 St. Louis Cardinals, 1988–1993 Phoenix Cardinals, 1994–present Arizona Cardinals

HOME STADIUM

University of Phoenix Stadium
1 Cardinals Drive
Glendale, AZ 85305

CAPACITY

63,400

OFFICIAL WEB SITE

www.azcardinals.com

FIRST GAME PLAYED

October 10, 1920

CHAMPIONSHIPS

NFL Champions 1925, 1947

SIGNATURE FOOD OF THE AREA

Southwestern

GREAT BARBECUE

Thee Pitts Again

GREAT STEAKHOUSE

Donovan's Steak and Chop House

GREAT BREW

Four Peaks 8th Street Ale

HALL OF FAMERS

Charles W. Bidwill Sr., Owner-Administrator, 1933–1947

Jimmy Conzelman, QB, 1940–1942, 1946–1948

Dan Dierdorf, OT, 1971–1983

John "Paddy" Driscoll, QB, 1920–1925

Dick "Night Train" Lane, CB, 1954–1959

Ollie Matson, HB, 1952, 1954–1958

Ernie Nevers, FB, 1929–1931

Jackie Smith, TE, 1963–1977

Charley Trippi, HB-QB, 1947–1955

Roger Wehrli, CB, 1969–1982

Larry Wilson, FS, 1960–1972

CHEERLEADERS

Cardinals Cheerleaders

BEST SEASON

1948 (11–1)

ARIZONA AND FOOD

The food of the Phoenix area surely has great Southwestern roots with spicy chiles, complex sauces, and tortillas as a huge part of most of the local diet. However, the area has grown so big and so fast that it's really become a melting pot of people and food cultures. The last time I was there, I had a very authentic Chicago hot dog and I saw many other transplanted regional restaurants and menus. I say you should enjoy the diversity and celebrate it for your Cardinals game-day meal. The climate will always dictate the foods that people eat in extreme places like the desert, so lighter fare is always a good idea. Of course just about anything is available in a big city like Phoenix, so you can enjoy fresh seafood in a place where there isn't much of it being harvested locally. They do grow lots of cantaloupes and other melons in Arizona, though, and a plate of those will make a great dessert. Be sure to have plenty of bottled water and soft drinks for your guests if your game-day party is outside, and stay out of the sun as much as possible so everyone will be safe and happy all the way to the end of the game.

Here are my suggestions for what to cook for a Cardinals Game-Day Party. Mix and match as you wish.

Grilled Avocado Halves (page 42)

Barbecued Chicken Nachos (page 52)

Fresh Breakfast Burritos (page 102)

Catfish Tacos with Citrus Salsa (page 134)

Spicy Spare Ribs (page 155)

Loaded Cornbread Casserole (page 208)

A plate of sliced fresh mixed melons

Preparing for the Game-Day Feast

MENU PLANNING

Just like an NFL coach, the game-day cook has to have a good plan in place if he expects to have a winning result. For us cooks, the winning result is a great spread of well-prepared food and a bunch of full and happy friends. I can't prove it, but I have a theory that the better the food at my party, the better my team will play. So this is important stuff. I've organized the recipes in this book into the major game-day food groups. They are Appetizers; Soups, Stews, and Chilies; Sandwiches; Entrées; Side Dishes; Desserts; and Drinks. I like to serve all of these as part of any game-day feast. If it's a hot day, I may skip the soup, but that sure is an important course on a cold day. I may use a couple of sandwich choices and skip the entrées if the time and facilities for the meal are limited, but I can usually make just about anything work with a little preplanning.

You'll notice that I always refer to lots of different food choices. It's my experience that the food on game day is best served as a day-long smorgasbord. We all like to graze anyway, and with this approach you can please even the pickiest palate. You'll see this throughout the book, but I truly believe that you should get some food out as soon as the gathering begins. Oftentimes it's early in the day and the guests haven't eaten anything yet, and oftentimes there are a few cocktails on the horizon, so they'll be looking to snack on something right away. I always make a salsa and get it out first in my team-logo helmet chip-and-dip server. Sometimes I add a homemade cheese dip or veggie dip with veggies and crackers. I don't mind adding in a store-bought cheese or deli tray either, as long as the quality is good. Then I like to get some sweets out, since there are always some guests with a sweet tooth that will start there. It can be cookies or brownies or the Sticky Fingers Cinnamon Bread (page 34) from the appetizer chapter, or even a plate of sweet rolls and donuts from your favorite bakery. If you're a West Coaster and your team is playing the early game, the Fresh Breakfast Burritos (page 102) or the Egg McDr. BBQ sandwiches (page 101) are going to be a great fit too. Mixing and matching is what this book is all about. Every game is a new, fun adventure and the food should be too.

While the guests are busy munching on the early offerings and deciding what the coaches should do to win the game, the cook has time to get the real food ready. If you're grilling appetizers, be sure to get them started right away. Everybody loves chicken wings, so I usually try to include at least one kind of those, and a vegetable appetizer goes well early in the day. If you're at a home, you may want to serve all of this at the beginning of the game and save the main courses for halftime or maybe even for after the game. There's usually a second game, you know. If you're at the game, you'll probably be starting early so serving the main course before you go into the stadium is a good fit. In that case, I make sure to have some sandwiches or something I can heat quickly for after the game. An exciting game can work up a fierce appetite and the traffic will be jammed anyway, so I say just serve up another meal.

When it comes to side dishes, I like to match them to the main course, but let's not overthink it. Hawaiian Fruit Salad (page 193) or Homemade Apple Slaw (page 194) go well with just about anything, especially if you're eating it in the parking lot. I like to make a lot of fun side dishes and the guests like to sample them all. This is a place where you can take a shortcut, too, and buy some of these premade. Just be sure to buy good quality.

Then comes the dessert. I like to make one main dessert that will be served at the end of the meal and a few of the aforementioned sweets to accompany it. Fresh fruits are always a nice add-on as well.

Last, but not least, are the refreshments. I always bring a cooler of mixed sodas—diet and regular—and some bottles of water. I also have another cooler full of beer. Beer is a game-day staple and many of the guests will enjoy it. If I know a guest or two has a certain soda or beer preference, I always try to accommodate them. I also like to offer a special drink of the day. Depending on the time of day and the location of the party, it may be a harmless drink like Homemade Lemonade (page 231) or Real Southern-Style Sweet Tea (page 231), but if there is a bus or plenty of designated drivers, it may be a Chocolate Martini (page 233) or Dr. BBQ's famous Parking Lot Punch (page 237).

Odds and Ends

Once you've got your menu in place, you'll need to map out a plan to get it all organized by game time. Shopping, prepping, and cooking ahead are always part of the plan, and if your game-day feast will be served in the parking lot you'll have the added tasks of packing all the gear and food for the trip. In either case, food safety is important and there are a few simple rules that can keep things in line:

//// Hot food must be kept hot (over 140°F).

//// Cold food must be kept cold (under 40°F).

//// Raw food and cooked food can NEVER share the same cooler, platter, cutting board, or knife unless a washing with hot soapy water and a thorough rinsing happens in between.

//// JUST WIPING IT OFF IS NOT OK!

//// Hands must be washed regularly with hot soapy water.

Some dishes need to be cooked ahead and there is nothing wrong with that, but the same safety rules apply. After cooking something, it must be kept hot until serving or be cooled quickly to be reheated later. For most food this can be done by spreading it out in a couple of shallow pans and refrigerating until cold. Then you can pack the food into zip-top bags or other sealed containers for travel, but it must remain refrigerated or on ice until it's time to reheat. Once the food is reheated, it must be kept hot if it won't be eaten immediately. This is best done in an electric food warmer or a Sterno-fueled chafing dish. Restaurant-grade chafing dishes are great for big crowds, can be found reasonably priced, and will last forever. As for the cold food, it must be kept very cold even during serving. This is easily done by placing the bowl or pan of food in a larger bowl or pan that's full of ice. You'll need to add some new ice once in a while if it's a warm day. Covering all food is a good idea too, and it's always best to keep it out of the sun if at all possible. Whew!

When the party is at the game, I like to use as many disposable items as possible, such as foil pans, paper plates, plastic cups, plastic tablecloths, and paper towels and napkins. Those Wet Nap towelettes in the cylinder are great too. This all helps with the dishwashing needs and makes clean-up back at home a lot easier. Heck, I've been known to use these things even if the party is at my house! Last but not least, don't forget the garbage bags. Feeding people creates a lot of garbage and it's part of the cook's job to make sure it all gets rounded up and taken away.

SAMPLE MENUS FOR SPECIAL OCCASIONS

Draft Day

You have to start somewhere, and this is how your team gets built—so why not have a little celebration for draft day? Besides, it's the off-season and a good excuse to get ready for some football. The day will revolve primarily around the couple of picks your team gets, so there's gonna be some free time in between. I'd suggest a few different grilled items done before and after your team picks.

Here's my draft-day menu:

Grilled Vidalia Onion Salsa (page 38)

Strawberry-Jalapeño Chicken Wings (page 50)

Grilled Tuna Sandwiches with Chipotle Mayo (page 135)

Rockin' London Broil (page 167)

Kitchen Sink Pasta Salad (page 192)

Chocolate-Apricot Tacos (page 224)

Minicamp

Technically this is just an excuse to have a few friends over, but occasionally something exciting happens at minicamp, like a fight among teammates or a guy missing his flight and arriving late, and you wouldn't want to hear about this on an empty stomach.

Here's my minicamp menu:

Nachos Ai Chihuahua (page 53)

Big Boy's Meatballs (page 64)

Barbecued Pulled Pork Sandwiches (page 108)

Krystal Quiche (page 148)

Spicy Tangy Slaw (page 194)

Barbecue Pit Beans (page 200)

Trish Trigg's Pecan Pie (page 213)

Preseason

Just like the teams, the fans need to get in shape for the season. Make this your practice run for some new dishes or techniques that you haven't tried yet so you'll have confidence when it's time to cook for the real thing.

Here's my preseason menu:

Asian Orange Wings (page 51)

Dr. BBQ's Grilled Shrimp Toast (page 57)

Ray's Favorite Lamb Chili (page 95)

Game-Day Chicken and Baby Corn Stir-Fry (page 180)

Parking Lot Pork Fried Rice (page 207)

Pear Cobbler with Raisins (page 219)

Opening Day

My high-school coach always told us that opening day was the biggest day of the season. I think that was because he knew we probably weren't going to make the playoffs, but I've always found opening day to be a grand celebration. The season is new, your best players are all there, and everyone is in the hunt for the championship. It's a great day for a party!

Here's my opening-day menu:

Screaming Yellow Salsa (page 39)

Garlic-Lovers' Cheese Dip (page 42)

Dr. BBQ's Grandma's Chicken Dumpling Soup (page 70)

Barbecued Bologna Sandwiches (page 110)

Peachy Baby Back Ribs (page 154)

Game-Day Caesar Salad (page 189)

Chipotle Pinto Beans (page 199)

Snickers-Stuffed Baked Apples (page 225)

Monday Night Football

My favorite thing about *Monday Night Football* has always been that I have the whole day to cook the meal, so I can really get serious. You only get one or two Monday night games for your team each year, so I always make it a special celebration.

Here's my Monday night menu:

Bloody Mary Chicken Wings (page 46)

Crabby Crab Cakes (page 62)

Dr. BBQ's Tailgate Gumbo (page 92)

Barbecued Brisket Sandwiches (page 109)

Barbecue Championship Rack of Lamb (page 159)

Kitchen Sink Pasta Salad (page 192)

Nancy P.'s Smoked Cheddar Double-Baked Potatoes (page 203)

White Chocolate–Granola-Macadamia Cookies (page 221)

The Playoffs

It's time to crank it up a little when the playoffs roll around. Your team had better bring their "A" game, and so should you. The stakes are high and the food should be up to the same level.

Here's my playoff menu:

Wing Ding Dry Rub Wings (page 47)

Grilled Scallops Wrapped in Bacon with Jalapeño Glaze (page 59)

Dr. BBQ's Championship Chili (page 98)

High-Octane Sloppy Joes (page 112)

Barbecued Chicken Legs with Raspberry-Chipotle Barbecue Sauce (page 176)

Baked Macaroni and Cheese (page 209)

Peachy Sweet Potato Pie (page 203)

Loaded Brownies (page 221)

The Super Bowl

The Super Bowl is the highlight of a game-day cook's season, especially if his team is playing in the big game. There's going to be a feast and it's going to last all day. The Super Bowl is the day to pull out all the stops and cook your best stuff, and lots of it. After all, the championship is on the line.

Here's my Super Bowl menu:

Sweet Sticky Barbecue Salsa with chips (page 38)

Barbecued Chicken Nachos (page 52)

Grilled Chili-Rubbed Shrimp Cocktail (page 56)

Grilled Mahi Mahi Skewers with Peppered Bacon (page 59)

Spicy Pepperoni-Stuffed Mushrooms (page 64)

Dr. BBQ's Grandma's Chicken Dumpling Soup (page 70)

Mac and Cheese Soup (page 74)

Italian Beef Sandwiches (page 104)

Grilled Carne Asada Tacos with Guacasalsa (page 132, 133)

Garlic-Infused Leg of Lamb (page 160)

Dr. BBQ's Lobster with Chile-Lime Butter (page 169)

Cheesy Deviled Eggs (page 187)

Game-Day Caesar Salad (page 189)

Double-Baked Potatoes with Gorgonzola (page 201)

Loaded Cornbread Casserole (page 208)

Trish Trigg's Pecan Pie (page 213)

White-Bottom Pumpkin Pie (page 213)

Key Lime Pie (page 214)

The Pro Bowl

The Pro Bowl is kind of laid-back, with being in Hawaii and all, and nobody really cares much who wins. It's really kind of a way to let everyone down slowly at the end of the NFL season. It's going to be a long off-season, and we all need one last game day to hold us over.

Here's my laid-back Pro Bowl menu:

Blue Cheese Veggie Dip with veggies (page 43)

Baked Brie with Chutney and Crisp Bacon (page 43)

Leftover Turkey Soup (page 83)

Ray's Tropical Pork Chop Sandwiches (page 140)

Fancy Crab and Swiss Quiche (page 148)

Tasty Salmon in a Package with Veggies (page 173)

Hawaiian Fruit Salad (page 193)

Peachy Sweet Potato Pie (page 203)

White Chocolate–Granola-Macadamia Cookies (page 221)

Atlanta Falcons

HOME STADIUM

The Georgia Dome
1 Georgia Dome Drive
Atlanta, GA 30313

CAPACITY

71,149

OFFICIAL WEB SITE

www.atlantafalcons.com

FIRST GAME PLAYED

September 11, 1966

CHAMPIONSHIPS

NFC Champions 1998

SIGNATURE FOOD OF THE AREA

Southern

GREAT BARBECUE

Fat Matt's Rib Shack

GREAT STEAKHOUSE

Bone's Restaurant

GREAT BREW

Terrapin Rye Pale Ale

HALL OF FAMERS

Eric Dickerson, RB, 1993

Tommy McDonald, WR, 1967

CHEERLEADERS

Falcons Cheerleaders

BEST SEASON

1998 (14–2)

ATLANTA AND FOOD

Atlanta is in the South, and real Southern food and hospitality abound, but it's also called the Capital of the New South in part because it has become so contemporary. The skyscrapers and big business make it a world-class city, and like all big cities, Atlanta has grown and diversified, but all of the Southern charm remains intact. Dining in Atlanta can range from a chili dog at The Varsity—which features carhops in bow ties—to the very Southern "meat and three" diners that are scattered throughout the city, to the trendy chef-based restaurants and bars of Buckhead. It's all quite different and I like to enjoy it all. Atlanta is home to my favorite grill company, Big Green Egg, so I always think about grilling and barbecue when I'm there. It's also the home of Coca-Cola and CNN. Be sure to get some fresh peaches if they're in season, too; they really are that good there. There's a lot to see, do, and eat in Atlanta, so it's easy to see why they call it "Hotlanta."

Here are my suggestions for what to cook for a Falcons Game-Day Party. Mix and match as you wish.

Peachy Keen Salsa (page 39)

Bloody Mary Chicken Wings (page 46)

Game-Day Smoky Chili (page 99)

Judy's Double-Stuffed Cheeseburgers (page 139)

Peachy Baby Back Ribs (page 154)

Double-Baked Potatoes with Gorgonzola (page 201)

BBQ-Rubbed Fruit Kabobs (page 206)

Harvey Wallbanger Cake (page 218)

Amazing Appetizers

You can't start a football game without a kickoff, and you can't start a game-day party without appetizers. To me the starters are the most important food of the day, and much like a team's first drive, they can set the tone for the day. If your party is anything like mine, the guests will arrive fired up for the game and hungry—so let's get them something good to start.

The appetizers for a game-day party can vary depending on the time of day the game is starting, so I've included some non-traditional choices here. For you West Coasters with an early game, it's going to be more like breakfast, or at least brunch, so a couple mellow choices like my homemade Sticky Fingers Cinnamon Bread (page 34) and Baked Brie with Chutney and Crisp Bacon (page 43) might be a nice start. If it's the pregame for *Monday Night Football*, it's going to be a little different. This will call for something a little rowdier like the Bloody Mary Chicken Wings (page 46) and the Screaming Yellow Salsa (page 39). Of course many football fans are just fine with chicken wings in the morning anyway, so I like to mix and match to please the whole crowd. If it's a bunch of your beer-drinking buddies, you can get hot and spicy and probably skip the veggie dip, but if the girls are coming, they might like the veggie dip and the cheese fondue.

In the spirit of dim sum or tapas, you could even exclusively serve appetizers during the whole game and have a successful meal. Just make many different kinds and many of them. Add a few bread choices and you've got an exciting game-day party. No matter how traditional or eclectic your spread is going to be, you'll want to include appetizers. I like to make at least two and usually three appetizers, plus a salsa to get them started. If you can get a little food in their hands early, then they'll let you prepare the rest of the food in peace, taking your time only to tell you how much they love the food, and that's a great way to start the game-day fun.

Banana-Cranberry-Walnut Muffins

A nice way to start and end game day.

½ cup (4 ounces) butter, at room temperature

1 cup sugar

2 large eggs, lightly beaten

2 large ripe bananas, mashed

2 cups all-purpose flour

1 teaspoon salt

1 teaspoon baking powder

½ teaspoon baking soda

⅓ cup buttermilk

½ cup chopped walnuts

½ cup dried cranberries

1 teaspoon vanilla extract

Preheat the oven to 400°F. Grease or line with paper a 12-muffin pan.

In a large bowl, beat together the butter and sugar until creamy. Add the eggs and bananas. Beat until fluffy. In another large bowl, combine the flour, salt, baking powder, and baking soda. Add to the creamed mixture. Add the buttermilk. Mix just until the dry ingredients are moistened. Stir in the walnuts, cranberries, and vanilla extract.

Divide the batter among the prepared muffin cups. Bake for 15 to 18 minutes, or until golden.

MAKES 12 MUFFINS

Sticky Fingers Cinnamon Bread

This is kind of a smashed-up pile of cinnamon rolls that the guests will be happy to pull apart. (Pictured on page 124.)

Baking spray for the pan

½ cup (4 ounces) butter

1 tablespoon ground cinnamon

1 cup sugar

Three 9.5-ounce tubes pull-apart biscuits (buy the small, cheap ones)

1 cup chopped pecans

1 cup butterscotch chips

¾ cup orange marmalade

Preheat the oven to 400°F. With baking spray, coat a 10-inch Bundt pan.

In a small microwave-safe dish in the microwave, melt the butter. In a small bowl, mix together the cinnamon and sugar. Using 1 tube, pull apart the biscuits and dip each one in the butter, then in the sugar mixture, and line the baking pan with them, laying them flat. Sprinkle with ⅓ of the pecans, ⅓ of the butterscotch pieces, and ¼ cup of the marmalade. Continue layering with the remaining 2 tubes of biscuits and the remaining pecans, chips, and marmalade.

Bake for 25 minutes, or until the top is golden and bubbly. Cool for 15 minutes. Invert the pan onto a serving plate. If the top biscuits stick, just pull them out of the pan and replace them on the loaf.

MAKES 8 SERVINGS

Banana-Nut Bread

A delicious way to use those bananas that are hanging around.

3 large bananas, very ripe

1 cup sugar

½ cup (4 ounces) butter, at room temperature

2 large eggs

1½ tablespoons buttermilk

1 teaspoon freshly squeezed lemon juice

2 cups all-purpose flour

1½ teaspoons baking powder

½ teaspoon baking soda

1 cup chopped walnuts

Preheat the oven to 350°F. Grease a 9-x-5-inch loaf pan.

Place the bananas, sugar, butter, eggs, buttermilk, and lemon juice in a blender container. Blend until smooth. In a large bowl, mix together the flour, baking powder, and baking soda. Pour the banana mixture over the flour mixture and stir just until the flour is moistened. Stir in the nuts.

Turn the mixture into the greased baking pan. Bake for 55 to 65 minutes, or until a wooden skewer inserted in the center comes out clean. Allow to cool for 5 minutes, then turn out onto a wire rack.

MAKES 8 SERVINGS

Beer Bread with Herbs

Everybody likes beer, bread, and herbs, so why not put them all together?

1 tablespoon vegetable shortening

3 tablespoons cornmeal

3 cups self-rising flour

¾ cup (3 ounces) freshly grated
Parmesan cheese

3 tablespoons sugar

1 tablespoon dried Italian herb blend

12 ounces dark beer, at room
temperature

2 tablespoons butter, at room
temperature

Preheat the oven to 325°F. Grease a 9-x-5-inch loaf pan with the shortening, and coat it with the cornmeal.

In a large bowl, combine the flour, Parmesan, sugar, and dried herbs. Mix well to combine. Stir in the beer to make a stiff batter.

Turn the batter into the prepared baking pan. Bake for 1 hour, or until a wooden skewer inserted in the center comes out clean. Heat the butter in a small dish in the microwave until it's melted. Allow the bread to cool for 5 minutes, then turn out onto a wire rack and brush the top with the melted butter.

MAKES 8 SERVINGS

Sweet Potato Bread with Pecans

Another great way to use sweet potatoes.

1½ cups mashed cooked sweet potatoes

3½ cups all-purpose flour

2 teaspoons baking powder

1 teaspoon baking soda

1 teaspoon salt

1 teaspoon ground cloves

1 teaspoon ground cinnamon

⅔ cup (5⅔ ounces) butter, at room temperature

1⅔ cups sugar

4 large eggs, lightly beaten

⅔ cup milk

1½ cups chopped pecans

Preheat the oven to 350°F. Grease two 9-x-5-inch loaf pans.

Press the cooked sweet potatoes through a sieve. In a medium bowl, sift together the flour, baking powder, baking soda, salt, cloves, and cinnamon. In a large mixing bowl, beat together the butter and sugar until creamy. Beat in the eggs until fluffy. Add the sweet potatoes and milk. Stir until blended. Add the flour mixture and mix thoroughly. Fold in the pecans.

Divide the batter evenly between the loaf pans. Bake for 1 hour, or until a wooden skewer inserted in the center comes out clean. Cool in pans on wire racks for 30 minutes.

MAKES 12 SERVINGS

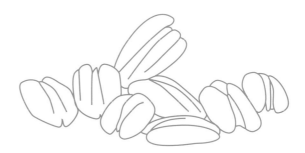

Sweet Sticky Barbecue Salsa

4 plum tomatoes, seeded and chopped

1 medium red onion, finely chopped

1 large green bell pepper, finely chopped

½ cup finely chopped celery

2 poblano peppers, roasted, peeled, and finely chopped

2 serrano chiles, finely chopped (remove the seeds if you like it mild)

1 jalapeño, finely chopped (remove the seeds if you like it mild)

¼ cup your favorite barbecue sauce

1 lime, juiced

1 tablespoon honey

1 clove garlic, crushed

1 teaspoon your favorite barbecue rub

This salsa is great with chips but it's also great spooned over chicken.

In a glass bowl, mix together all of the ingredients. Refrigerate for 30 minutes. Mix again and serve with tortilla chips.

MAKES ABOUT 2 CUPS

Grilled Vidalia Onion Salsa

2 poblano chiles

1 large Vidalia onion

2 tablespoons olive oil

2 medium tomatoes, seeded and diced

½ red bell pepper, diced small

¼ cup chopped fresh cilantro

Juice of 2 limes

1 jalapeño, finely chopped

Salt, as needed

The sweet grilled onion really makes this salsa special.

Prepare the grill for cooking over direct high heat.

Roast the poblanos until they are blistered on all sides, then set them aside in a covered container. Peel the onion and cut it into ¾-inch slabs. Brush the slices with oil and grill until browned and soft, flipping occasionally. This should take 8 to 10 minutes total. Let cool.

Peel and chop the poblanos and put them in a medium bowl. Chop the onion and add it to the bowl. Add the tomatoes, pepper, cilantro, lime juice, and jalapeño. Mix well. Let rest for 15 minutes and mix again. Add salt as needed and mix again.

MAKES 2 CUPS

1 red bell pepper, roasted, peeled, and chopped

1 yellow bell pepper, roasted, peeled, and chopped

3 thick slices sweet onion, lightly grilled and chopped

2 ears fresh sweet corn, oiled, grilled, and cut from the cob

1 head garlic, roasted, peeled, and finely chopped

2 yellow tomatoes, seeded and chopped

1 medium carrot, grated

2 limes, juiced

1 habanero chile, seeded and finely chopped (these are insanely hot and should only be handled while wearing food-service gloves)

1 teaspoon coarse ground black pepper

1 teaspoon white vinegar

Salt, as needed

Screaming Yellow Salsa

This salsa looks cool and mild but the taste is hot and wild. It's great with tortilla chips but also good spooned over grilled fish.

In a large glass bowl, combine all the ingredients. Toss well and let rest for 30 minutes. Toss again and refrigerate for at least 2 hours and preferably overnight. Check for salt and add if necessary before serving.

MAKES 2 CUPS

Two 10-ounce cans Ro-Tel diced tomatoes with green chiles

2 large peaches, pitted and cut into small dice

1 small red onion, finely chopped

2 jalapeños, finely chopped

¼ cup chopped fresh cilantro

1 lime, juiced

2 cloves garlic, crushed

½ teaspoon ground black pepper

½ teaspoon salt, or more as needed

Peachy Keen Salsa

Like so many salsas, this peachy version is great with chips but also goes well over grilled pork chops.

In a large glass bowl, mix together all the ingredients. Combine well. Cover with plastic wrap and refrigerate for 1 hour. Mix well, taste for salt, and add if needed.

MAKES 2 CUPS

Carolina Panthers

HOME STADIUM

Bank of America Stadium
800 South Mint Street
Charlotte, NC 28202

CAPACITY

73,298

OFFICIAL WEB SITE

www.panthers.com

FIRST GAME PLAYED

September 3, 1995

CHAMPIONSHIPS

NFC Champions 2003

SIGNATURE FOOD OF THE AREA

Barbecue

GREAT BARBECUE

Big Bob Gibson's Bar-B-Q

GREAT STEAKHOUSE

Beef n' Bottle

GREAT BREW

There's nothing local. Go to The Flying Saucer and order what you like.

HALL OF FAMERS

Reggie White, DE, 2000

CHEERLEADERS

Top Cats

BEST SEASON

1996 (12–4)

CHARLOTTE AND FOOD

North Carolina is barbecue country. Pork barbecue—big, giant hunks of pork being cooked over real wood. Not too many ribs or beef briskets around here. It's about pork shoulders and whole hogs. North Carolina is about pork barbecue served with slaw and a little vinegar sauce and not much else. Like most of the fast-growing cities that have NFL teams, Charlotte has been influenced heavily by all the transplanted folks from around the country who bring new things to town, but it hasn't changed things much. It remains a nice Southern city with nice Southern people who love barbecue. You'll have no trouble finding a Southern-style diner that will have great food and probably some very good pies, but don't be surprised if they also have barbecue on the menu. It won't be some frozen barbecue either; they'll have a pit house out back and there will be some pork cooking. It's just the way of life there. Have the barbecue and enjoy it.

Here are my suggestions for what to cook for a Panthers Game-Day Party. Mix and match as you wish.

Sweet Potato Bread with Pecans (page 37)

Wing Ding Dry Rub Wings (page 47)

Mac and Cheese Soup (page 74)

Barbecued Pulled Pork Sandwiches (page 108)

Maple Pork on a Maple Plank (page 151)

Spicy Tangy Slaw (page 194)

Barbecue Pit Beans (page 200)

Sweet Blueberry-Apricot Crumble (page 227)

Grilled Avocado Halves

I was in a grocery store in California one day and I saw a package of beautiful frozen avocado halves. So I bought them and we were eating this dish a short time later.

Three 12-inch flour tortillas, cut into quarters

Olive oil, as needed

Good-quality chili powder, as needed

12 peeled and pitted avocado halves, fresh or frozen and defrosted

1 cup salsa

½ cup (2 ounces) shredded Jack cheese

Prepare the grill for cooking over direct medium heat.

Brush the tortilla quarters lightly with the oil. Sprinkle them lightly with the chili powder. On top of each tortilla quarter, place an avocado half. Fill the pit cavity with salsa. Place the tortillas with the avocado halves directly on the grill and cook for 5 minutes. Top with the cheese, cover the grill, and cook another 5 minutes, or until the cheese is melted. Carefully remove the tortillas to plates and serve.

MAKES 12 SERVINGS

Garlic-Lovers' Cheese Dip

Lots of good roasted garlic in this dip.

4 ounces cream cheese, cut into cubes

8 ounces sharp Cheddar cheese, shredded

½ cup beer (whatever you're drinking)

4 slices bacon, cooked and crumbled

6 cloves roasted garlic, finely chopped

1 tablespoon Cholula hot sauce

1 teaspoon dry mustard

½ teaspoon cayenne

2 green onions, sliced

Crackes, for serving

Put the 2 cheeses in a glass bowl and microwave on high for 2 minutes. Add the beer and mix well. Heat for about another 2 minutes, or until the cheese is melted. Mix until well blended. Add the bacon, garlic, hot sauce, dry mustard, and cayenne. Mix until well blended. Microwave for 1 more minute. Stir well and transfer to a serving bowl or crock. Refrigerate for at least 2 hours. Garnish with the green onions and serve with crackers.

MAKES 1½ CUPS

1 large Granny Smith apple, diced

1 medium onion, diced

½ red bell pepper, chopped

½ cup sugar

⅓ cup cider vinegar

¼ cup water

1 tablespoon balsamic vinegar

1 tablespoon minced garlic

¾ cup chopped dried apricots

½ cup raisins

2 teaspoons grated peeled fresh ginger

1½ teaspoons mustard seeds

¼ teaspoon cayenne

¼ teaspoon salt

One 16-ounce round Brie

12 slices bacon, cooked crisp and chopped

Crusty bread or crackers, for serving

Baked Brie with Chutney and Crisp Bacon

The bacon and the homemade chutney really make this baked Brie a winner.

To make the chutney, in a large saucepan over medium-high heat, combine the apple, onion, pepper, sugar, cider vinegar, water, balsamic vinegar, and garlic. Bring to a boil and reduce to a low simmer. Cook for 15 minutes, stirring occasionally. Add the apricots and remaining chutney ingredients and continue cooking until the mixture thickens slightly and becomes syrupy, about 35 minutes. Remove from the heat and cool. This can be made the day ahead and refrigerated.

Preheat the oven to 350°F or prepare the grill for cooking over indirect medium heat. Place the Brie in a ceramic baking dish or aluminum-foil pan. Heap the chutney over and around the Brie. Bake or grill, covered, for 15 minutes, or until the Brie begins to melt. Top with the chopped bacon. Serve with crusty bread or crackers.

MAKES 8 SERVINGS

8 ounces blue cheese, crumbled

½ cup chopped pecans

¼ cup whipping cream, or more as needed

1 cup sour cream

2 tablespoon finely chopped fresh chives

1 teaspoon freshly grated lemon zest

Blue Cheese Veggie Dip

This dip is a great way to start a game day. It will keep them busy while you get the rest of the food prepared. Serve with plenty of washed fresh veggies. I like to use carrots, broccoli, mushrooms, and celery sticks.

In a medium bowl, combine the cheese, pecans, and ¼ cup whipping cream with a wooden spoon until well blended. Mix in the sour cream, chives, and lemon zest. Add a little more whipping cream to smooth the dip out if needed. Cover and refrigerate until needed.

MAKES 2½ CUPS

Chicago Bears

HOME STADIUM

Soldier Field
1410 South Museum Campus Drive
Chicago, IL 60605

CAPACITY

66,944

OFFICIAL WEB SITE

www.chicagobears.com

FIRST GAME PLAYED

October 3, 1920

CHAMPIONSHIPS

NFL/NFC Champions 1921, 1932, 1933, 1940, 1941, 1943, 1946, 1963, 1985, 2006
Super Bowl Champions 1985

SIGNATURE FOOD OF THE AREA

Italian beef sandwich

GREAT BARBECUE

Honey 1

GREAT STEAKHOUSE

Gibsons

GREAT BREW

Goose Island Honkers Ale

HALL OF FAMERS

Doug Atkins, WR, 1955–1966
George Blanda, QB/PK, 1949–1958
Dick Butkus, LB, 1965–1973

Guy Chambers, E, 1920–1921
George Connor, T, 1948–1955
Jimmy Conzelman, RB, 1920
Mike Ditka, TE, 1961–1966
Paddy Driscoll, RB, 1920, 1926–1929
Jim Finks, GM, 1974–1983
Danny Fortmann, G, 1936–1943
Bill George, G/LB, 1952–1965
Red Grange, RB, 1925, 1929–1934
George Halas, E, 1920–1929; Coach, 1920–1929, 1933–1942, 1946–1955, 1958–1967; Owner, 1920–1983
Dan Hampton, DE, 1979–1990
Ed Healey, T, 1922–1927
Bill Hewitt, E, 1932–1936
Stan Jones, T, 1954–1965
Walt Kiesling, G, 1934
Bobby Layne, QB, 1948
Sid Luckman, QB, 1939–1950
Link Lyman, T, 1926–1928, 1930–1931, 1933–1934
George McAfee, RB, 1940–1941, 1945–1950
George Musso, G, 1933–1944
Bronko Nagurski, FB, 1930–1937, 1943
Alan Page, DT, 1978–1981
Walter Payton, RB, 1975–1987
Gale Sayers, RB, 1965–1971
Mike Singletary, LB, 1981–1992
George Trafton, C, 1920–1932
Clyde Turner, C, 1940–1952

CHEERLEADERS

None

BEST SEASON

1985 (15–1)

CHICAGO AND FOOD

I'm a little biased because I lived there most of my life, but I think Chicago is the best food city anywhere. People think that Chicagoans eat deep-dish pizza all the time. But that's really not accurate. In the neighborhoods, the pizza is thin and delicious. Besides, I consider Italian beef to be the signature dish of Chicago. It's what the locals eat every day. Don't forget the hot dogs either. They are a staple of the typical Chicago diet. I gotta tell you, those Da Bears guys on *SNL* were pretty much on the money. Chicago has great ethnic diversity as well, so the food in Greektown is great and a big part of the city. Don't skip all the independent Italian restaurants and the Polish and German and Jewish and Czech and about every other cuisine you can think of. There are also some great chefs that make Chicago their home and they've had a big influence on the cuisine, but it all fits together nicely.

Here are my suggestions for what to cook for a Bears Game-Day Party. Mix and match as you wish.

Nachos Ai Chihuahua (page 53)

Spicy Sausage Bread (page 63)

Italian Sausage Soup (page 75)

Italian Beef Sandwiches (page 104)

Tofu Eggless Egg Salad Sandwiches (just kidding)

Grilled Sirloin Steak with Two-Mushroom Sauté (page 166)

Lettuce and Tomato Wedges with Creamy Blue Cheese (page 192)

Zesty Roasted Garlic Mashed Potatoes (page 200)

Cupcakes with blue frosting and an orange C on top

Bloody Mary Chicken Wings

I had this idea in the middle of the night. It's a hit with the game-day crowd.
(Pictured on page 114.)

15 whole, fresh
chicken wings

BLOODY MARY RUB

2 tablespoons celery salt

1 tablespoon good-quality chili powder

1 teaspoon black pepper

1 teaspoon granulated onion

1 teaspoon granulated garlic

1 teaspoon brown sugar

½ teaspoon cayenne

BLOODY MARY SAUCE

1½ cups V-8 juice

3 tablespoons Worcestershire sauce

3 tablespoons Tabasco Garlic Sauce

1 lemon, juiced

1 teaspoon salt

Prepared horseradish (optional)

Russian vodka for serving

Celery sticks for serving

With a sharp knife, cut the tips off the chicken wings and save the tips for stock. Slash the inside of each wing joint to help them cook more evenly, but don't cut them all the way through.

In a small bowl, mix together the rub ingredients. Sprinkle over the chicken wings, coating them evenly.

Prepare the grill for cooking over direct medium heat. Grill the wings, turning often, for 30 minutes, or until the wings are crispy and golden.

Meanwhile, mix the sauce ingredients together and set aside. Put the vodka in the freezer.

Transfer the wings to an aluminum-foil pan. Pour the sauce over the wings, tossing to coat. Put the pan on the grill. Cover the grill and cook for another 30 minutes, tossing the wings after 15 minutes to coat. If the pan goes dry, add a small amount of beer to keep it from burning. Remove the wings to a plate, and drizzle with the sauce if there is any left. Serve with celery sticks and shots of ice-cold vodka.

MAKES 15 SERVINGS

Wing Ding Dry Rub Wings

This great and simple wing recipe has won some grilling contest awards.

15 whole, fresh chicken wings

WING DING DRY RUB

1 tablespoon granulated garlic

1 tablespoon granulated onion

1 tablespoon good-quality chili powder

1 tablespoon lemon pepper

1 tablespoon salt

1 tablespoon turbinado sugar
(Sugar in the Raw)

1 teaspoon ground cumin

1 teaspoon paprika

1 teaspoon cayenne

With a sharp knife, cut the tips off the chicken wings and save the tips for stock. Slash the inside of each wing joint to help them cook more evenly, but don't cut them all the way through.

In a small bowl, mix together the rub ingredients. Sprinkle over the chicken wings, coating them evenly.

Prepare the grill for cooking over direct medium heat. Grill the wings, turning often, for 30 minutes, or until they are nicely browned and the juices run clear. You may serve the wings whole or cut them into single-joint segments.

MAKES 15 SERVINGS

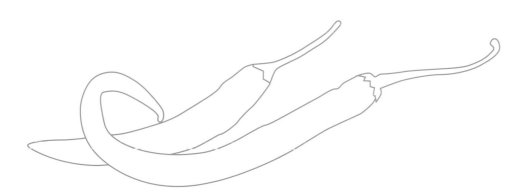

Dallas Cowboys

HOME STADIUM

Texas Stadium
2401 E. Airport Freeway
Irving, TX 75062

CAPACITY

65,595

OFFICIAL WEB SITE

www.dallascowboys.com

FIRST GAME PLAYED

September 24, 1960

CHAMPIONSHIPS

NFC Champions 1970, 1971, 1975,
1977, 1978, 1992, 1993, 1995

Super Bowl Champions 1971, 1977,
1992, 1993, 1995

SIGNATURE FOOD OF THE AREA

Chicken-fried steak

GREAT BARBECUE

Railhead

GREAT STEAKHOUSE

Bob's Steak and Chop House

GREAT BREW

Shiner Bock

HALL OF FAMERS

Herb Adderley, DB, 1970–1972
Troy Aikman, QB, 1989–2000
Lance Alworth, WR, 1971–1972
Mike Ditka, TE, 1969–1972
Tony Dorsett, RB, 1977–1987
Forrest Gregg, OT, 1971
Michael Irvin, WR, 1988–1999
Tom Landry, Coach, 1960–1988
Bob Lilly, DT, 1961–1974
Tommy McDonald, WR, 1964
Mel Renfro, DB, 1964–1977
Tex Schramm, President, 1960–1988
Jackie Smith, TE, 1978
Roger Staubach, QB, 1969–1979
Randy White, DT, 1975–1988
Rayfield Wright, OT, 1967–1979

CHEERLEADERS

Dallas Cowboys Cheerleaders

BEST SEASONS

1992, 2007 (13–3)

DALLAS AND FOOD

While I consider chicken-fried steak to be the signature dish of Dallas, Mexican food and Tex-Mex are well represented there and so is barbe-cue. I'd say all three are alive and well and represent what Dallas is. The mix of Mexican and cowboy food truly represents Dallas as well as much of Texas. Dallas food isn't influenced very much by the people who move there. Texans love being in Texas, and they are proud to be there. They're not looking to change much of anything about Texas. Even the upscale restaurants serve some fancy version of these favorites. I've heard of a restaurant serving a Kobe beef chicken-fried steak, and they serve barbecue at The Mansion on Turtle Creek. It doesn't get any more uptown than that. Most of the barbecue restaurants are a little more downtown, though. Railhead and Angelo's are two of the best barbecue joints in the area, and they both take pride in serving really cold beer in heavy glass schooners. I think that's a good thing.

Here are my suggestions for what to cook for a Cowboys Game-Day Party. Mix and match as you wish.

Grilled Vidalia Onion Salsa (page 38)

Stuffed Jalapeños Wrapped in Bacon (page 63)

Dr. BBQ's Championship Chili (page 98)

Barbecued Brisket Sandwiches (page 109)

Gringo Huevos Rancheros (page 147)

Chipotle Pinto Beans (page 199)

Grilled Grits (page 208)

Chocolate-Apricot Tacos (page 224)

Strawberry-Jalapeño Chicken Wings

The sweet strawberry preserves and the spicy jalapeños go very well together in this dish.

15 fresh, whole chicken wings

Your favorite barbecue rub, as needed

STRAWBERRY-JALAPEÑO GLAZE

1 cup strawberry preserves

½ cup chopped pickled sliced jalapeño (from the jar)

Juice of 1 lime

2 tablespoons Jack Daniel's whiskey

With a sharp knife, cut the tips off the chicken wings and save the tips for stock. Slash the inside of each wing joint to help them cook more evenly, but don't cut them all the way through. Sprinkle liberally with the dry rub.

Prepare the grill for cooking over direct medium heat. In a small saucepan, warm the preserves and add the jalapeño and lime juice. Cook over low heat for 5 minutes. Remove from the heat and stir in the whiskey. Grill the wings, turning often, for 30 minutes, or until they are nicely browned and the juices run clear. You may serve the wings whole or cut them into single-joint segments.

Transfer the wings to a bowl. If necessary, warm the glaze just to loosen it up and then pour it over the wings. Toss to coat well and serve.

MAKES 15 SERVINGS

Asian Orange Wings

This recipe started with a good name and grew from there.

15 fresh, whole chicken wings.

Your favorite barbecue rub, as needed

ASIAN ORANGE GLAZE

1 cup orange marmalade

2 tablespoons hoisin sauce

1 tablespoon plus 1 teaspoon soy sauce
(I like Kikkoman)

1 tablespoon rice vinegar

1 tablespoon "rooster" (sriracha)
chili sauce

With a sharp knife, cut the tips off the chicken wings and save the tips for stock. Slash the inside of each wing joint to help them cook more evenly, but don't cut them all the way through. Sprinkle liberally with the dry rub, coating them evenly.

Prepare the grill for cooking over direct medium heat. In a small saucepan, warm the marmalade and add the hoisin, soy sauce, vinegar, and rooster sauce. Cook over low heat for 5 minutes. Remove from the heat. Grill the wings, turning often, for 30 minutes, or until they are nicely browned and the juices run clear. You may serve the wings whole or cut them into single-joint segments.

Transfer the wings to a bowl. If necessary, warm the glaze just to loosen it up and then pour it over the wings. Toss to coat well and serve.

MAKES 15 SERVINGS

Barbecued Chicken Nachos

A great way to use that leftover chicken.

¼ cup oil

1 large onion, halved and sliced

1 pound restaurant-style tortilla chips

3 cups diced cooked chicken

2 cups your favorite barbecue sauce

1 cup (4 ounces) finely shredded Cheddar cheese

1 cup (4 ounces) finely shredded Jack cheese

¼ cup chopped fresh cilantro

In a large skillet, heat the oil over medium-high heat. Add the onion and cook, stirring occasionally, until soft and golden brown. Transfer to a paper towel to cool.

Preheat the oven to 350°F or prepare the grill for cooking over indirect medium heat.

Place the chips in a large aluminum-foil pan. In a medium bowl, mix the chicken and the barbecue sauce. Pour the chicken and sauce over the chips, spreading them evenly. Top with the onions and then with the cheeses. Put the pan in the oven or on the grill with the lid closed for 10 minutes, or until the cheeses are melted and the chips are warm. Top with the cilantro to serve.

MAKES 10 SERVINGS

Nachos Ai Chihuahua

These can be as hot or as mild as you like. Just add or subtract some of the hot sauce and add or subtract the jalapeño slices. I use a middle-of-the-road hot sauce like Frank's. Beware if you're using one of those blazing exotic hot sauces.

1 pound restaurant-style tortilla chips

1 pound Velveeta, cubed

One 15-ounce can chili with beans

One 15-ounce can chili without beans

2 tablespoons hot sauce (more or less to taste)

½ cup pickled sliced jalapeños (from the jar), drained

½ cup sliced green onions

Preheat the oven to 350°F or prepare the grill for cooking over indirect medium heat.

Place the chips in a large aluminum-foil pan. In a medium saucepan, heat the Velveeta and the 2 kinds of chili until everything is melted and well blended. Mix in the hot sauce. Pour over the chips. Put the pan in the oven or on the grill with the lid closed, for 5 minutes. Remove and top with the jalapeño slices and the green onions to serve.

MAKES 10 SERVINGS

Three-Bean Nachos

These are a nice change of pace and good for the vegetarian crowd. If they don't eat dairy either, just skip the cheese or use soy cheese instead.

One 15-ounce can navy beans, drained

One 15-ounce can black beans, drained

One 15-ounce can chili beans in sauce

1 pound restaurant-style tortilla chips

2 cups (1 pound) shredded mixed Cheddar and Jack cheeses

1 cup shredded lettuce

1 cup diced tomato

1 cup chopped onion

Preheat the oven to 350°F or prepare the grill for cooking over indirect medium heat.

In a medium bowl, combine the navy, black, and chili beans. Place the chips in a large aluminum-foil pan. Top with the beans, spreading them evenly. Top with the cheese. Put the pan in the oven or on the grill with the lid closed for 10 to 15 minutes, or until the cheese is melted and the chips and beans are warm. Top with the lettuce, tomato, and onion to serve.

MAKES 10 SERVINGS

Detroit Lions

HOME STADIUM

Ford Field
2000 Brush Street
Detroit, MI 48226

CAPACITY

65,000

OFFICIAL WEB SITE

www.detroitlions.com

FIRST GAME PLAYED

September 23, 1934

CHAMPIONSHIPS

NFL Champions 1935, 1952, 1953, 1957

SIGNATURE FOOD OF THE AREA

Coney Dogs

GREAT BARBECUE

Slows Bar BQ

GREAT STEAKHOUSE

Carl's Chop House

GREAT BREW

Atwater Block Brewery

HALL OF FAMERS

Lem Barney, CB, 1967–1977
Jack Christensen, B, 1951–1958
Earl Clark, QB, 1931–1932,
1934–1938
Lou Creekmur, T, 1950–1959
Bill Dudley, RB, 1947–1949
Frank Gatski, C, 1957
John Henry Johnson, RB, 1957–1959
Dick Lane, DB, 1960–1965
Yale Lary, DB, 1952–1953,
1956–1964
Bobby Layne, QB, 1950–1958
Ollie Matson, RB, 1963
Hugh McElhenny, RB, 1964
Barry Sanders, RB, 1989–1998
Charlie Sanders, TE, 1968–1977
Joe Schmidt, LB, 1953–1965
Doak Walker, HB, 1950–1955
Alex Wojciechowicz, C, 1938–1946

CHEERLEADERS

None

BEST SEASON

1991 (12–4)

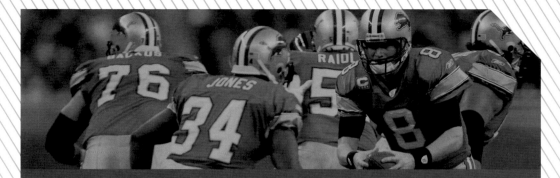

DETROIT AND FOOD

When it comes to the NFL and a game-day get-together in Detroit, you can't help but think about Thanksgiving dinner. Since the tradition started in 1934, Detroit Lions fans have been watching their team play on Thanksgiving Day and that means turkey and football for all the fans in Detroit. Detroit has succumbed to suburban sprawl like so many of the big northern cities, and the suburbs abound with the big chain restaurants, but there are plenty of good pizza parlors in Detroit, some serious soul food, and there are the famous Coney Dog stands, where they serve wonderful Coney Island—style chili dogs. It may seem a little out of place, but this has been a popular item in Detroit for decades. But when I go to Detroit for football, I want to see a turkey cooking and some mashed potatoes and gravy. John Madden has immortalized many great players with a turkey leg award for being the MVP after the Thanksgiving Day game, but those legs never get to the trophy case of the player. Who can resist a turkey leg on Thanksgiving?

Here are my suggestions for what to cook for a Lions Game-Day Party. Mix and match as you wish.

Spicy Pepperoni-Stuffed Mushrooms (page 64)

Stuffed Potato Skins (page 65)

Dr. BBQ's Grandma's Chicken Dumpling Soup (page 70)

Scottie's Fried Turkey (page 182)

Turkey Gravy Sandwiches with Homemade Cranberry Sauce (page 138)

Zesty Roasted Garlic Mashed Potatoes (page 200)

Peachy Sweet Potato Pie (page 203)

White-Bottom Pumpkin Pie (page 213)

Grilled Chili-Rubbed Shrimp Cocktail

You'll never boil a shrimp or use bottled cocktail sauce again.

24 jumbo raw shrimp, peeled and deveined

16 bamboo skewers soaked in water for 1 hour

CHILI RUB

1 tablespoon good-quality chili powder

½ teaspoon ground cinnamon

½ teaspoon dried oregano

Pinch of salt

COCKTAIL SAUCE

1 cup prepared chili sauce

¼ cup prepared horseradish

Juice of 1 lemon

Pinch of cayenne (optional)

1 lemon, thinly sliced

Prepare the grill for cooking over direct medium-high heat. Prepare a big bowl of ice for cooling the shrimp after cooking. Skewer the shrimp, 3 at a time, and doubling up the skewers to make a ladder effect.

To prepare the rub, combine the ingredients in a small bowl and mix together. Sprinkle the rub over the shrimp on both sides. Grill the shrimp for 3 to 4 minutes on each side, or until they are opaque. When the shrimp are done, slide them off of the skewers into the bowl of ice. Toss the shrimp with the ice to cool them and stop the cooking process. When the shrimp are cool, transfer them to a plate covered with paper towels. Refrigerate for 30 minutes.

To prepare the sauce, combine the ingredients in a small bowl and whisk them together. Serve 6 shrimp per guest with a dollop of sauce and a few lemon slices.

MAKES 4 SERVINGS

Dr. BBQ's Grilled Shrimp Toast

You can leave these sandwiches intact and serve them for a delicious lunch if you like.

8 ounces any size raw shrimp, peeled and deveined

2 large egg whites

2 cloves garlic, roasted and minced

1 tablespoon sherry

½ teaspoon minced peeled fresh ginger

¼ teaspoon salt

¼ teaspoon white pepper

12 slices sandwich bread, crust removed

Olive oil, as needed

Good-quality chili powder, as needed

Prepare the grill for cooking over direct medium heat.

Mince the shrimp. Add them to a bowl with the egg whites, garlic, sherry, ginger, salt, and pepper. Mix well and set aside. Line a baking sheet with waxed paper. Brush one side of each of the slices of bread lightly with olive oil. Sprinkle the oiled side lightly with chili powder. Lay 6 of the slices oiled-sides down on the waxed paper. Evenly distribute the shrimp mixture among the 6 slices of bread, spreading the mixture to the edges. Top with the remaining bread, oiled-sides up. Top the cooking grate with aluminum foil. Grill the shrimp toast directly on the foil until golden brown. Turn and grill the other sides until golden brown. Remove to a cutting board and cut each sandwich into 4 triangles.

MAKES 24 SERVINGS

Grilled Scallops Wrapped in Bacon with Jalapeño Glaze

The spicy jalapeño glaze makes these a real treat.

12 large sea scallops

12 slices bacon

2 tablespoons butter

3 tablespoons jalapeño hot sauce

Prepare the grill for cooking over direct medium heat.

Using a whole slice of bacon per scallop, wrap the bacon under the bottom and over the top of each scallop, repeating until it's all wrapped. Secure with a toothpick in the front. (This way the bacon is on the direct heat so it gets cooked while it's protecting the tender flesh of the scallop.) Place the scallops directly on the grill. Cook until the bacon is browned and cooked on the bottom. Flip and cook until the other side of the bacon is browned and done. The total cooking time should be about 12 minutes. Remove to a plate and let rest for 3 minutes.

Meanwhile, melt the butter and mix it with the hot sauce. Drizzle it over the scallops.

MAKES 12 SERVINGS

Grilled Mahi Mahi Skewers with Peppered Bacon

I served these at a winemaker's dinner in Florida and the guests loved them.

1 pound boneless mahi mahi fillet

6 slices peppered bacon, cut in half

12 bamboo skewers soaked in water for 1 hour

Prepare the grill for cooking over direct medium heat.

Cut the fillet into 12 even pieces. Wrap each piece in one half slice of bacon, securing the bacon with the tip of a skewer as you spear the mahi. Keep the wrapped mahi at the top of the skewer like a lollipop. Grill the wrapped skewers for about 6 minutes per side, or until the bacon is brown and crispy.

MAKES 12 SERVINGS

Green Bay Packers

HOME STADIUM

Lambeau Field
1265 Lombardi Avenue
Green Bay, WI 54304

CAPACITY

72,569

OFFICIAL WEB SITE

www.packers.com

FIRST GAME PLAYED

September 14, 1919

CHAMPIONSHIPS

NFL/NFC Champions 1929, 1930, 1931, 1936, 1939, 1944, 1961, 1962, 1965, 1966, 1967, 1996, 1997

Super Bowl Champions 1966, 1967, 1996

SIGNATURE FOOD OF THE AREA

Bratwurst

GREAT BARBECUE

You're gonna have to make your own.

GREAT STEAKHOUSE

Brett Favre's Steakhouse

GREAT BREW

Old Style

HALL OF FAMERS

Herb Adderley, DB, 1961–1969
Tony Canadeo, RB, 1941–1944, 1946–1952
Willie Davis, DE, 1960–1969
Len Ford, DE, 1958
Forrest Gregg, OT, 1956, 1958–1970
Ted Hendricks, LB, 1974
Arnie Herber, QB, 1930–1940
Clarke Hinkle, FB, 1932–1941
Paul Hornung, RB, 1957–1962, 1964–1966
Cal Hubbard, OT, 1929–1933, 1935
Don Hutson, WR, 1935–1945
Henry Jordan, DT, 1959–1969
Walt Kiesling, G, 1935–1936
Curly Lambeau, Coach, 1919–1949
James Lofton, WR, 1978–1986
Vince Lombardi, Coach, 1959–1968
John McNally, RB, 1929–1933, 1935–1936
Mike Michalske, G, 1929–1935, 1937
Ray Nitschke, LB, 1958–1972
Jim Ringo, C, 1953–1963
Bart Starr, QB, 1956–1971
Jan Stenerud, PK, 1980–1983
Jim Taylor, FB, 1958–1966
Emlen Tunnell, S, 1959–1961
Reggie White, DE, 1993–1998
Willie Wood, S, 1960–1971

CHEERLEADERS

None

BEST SEASON

1962 (13–1)

GREEN BAY AND FOOD

Green Bay is a meat and potatoes town. Make that meat and potatoes and cheese. And if the meat is in the form of a bratwurst, all the better. I get mad when I go somewhere and find that the writings about the food in that town don't match up with what's really going on. This is not a problem in Green Bay, or any other place in Wisconsin for that matter. They love bratwurst, beer, and cheese and are proud of it. A TV station in Madison holds a "Take Your Brat to Work" day where you drive through a parking lot in the morning and buy a couple bratwursts to take to work for your lunch. It's a rousing success too! On Friday nights, the folks in Wisconsin go out for fish fry. Almost everyone I know in Wisconsin participates in this, and when I'm there, so do I. Many of the restaurants offer a fairly priced all-you-can-eat version that's my favorite. Then on Sunday, you grill up some brats and drink a few beers and life is good.

Here are my suggestions for what to cook for a Packers Game-Day Party. Mix and match as you wish.

Garlic-Lovers' Cheese Dip (page 42)

Big Boy's Meatballs (page 64)

Mac and Cheese Soup (page 74)

Bratwurst with Beer, Butter, and Onions (page 129)

Fish Fry with Hush Puppies (page 172)

Cheesy Deviled Eggs (page 187)

Warm German Potato Salad (page 195)

A big cake with the Packers' logo on it

Crabby Crab Cakes

These are pretty simple and all about the crab. There's no need to change things that work.

2 large eggs

2 large egg whites

½ cup chopped celery

½ cup chopped green onion

1 teaspoon minced garlic

1 teaspoon hot sauce

¼ teaspoon freshly grated lemon zest

12 ounces jumbo lump crabmeat

1 cup crushed oyster crackers

½ cup dried bread crumbs

¼ cup all-purpose flour

¼ teaspoon salt

¼ teaspoon paprika

⅓ cup olive oil

In a large bowl, whisk together the whole eggs and egg whites until frothy. Stir in the celery, green onion, garlic, hot sauce, and lemon zest. Gently fold in the crabmeat, oyster crackers, and bread crumbs until evenly mixed. Set aside.

On a plate, mix together the flour, salt, and paprika. Divide the crab mixture into 6 mounds, form into balls, then roll them in the flour mixture; place on a platter. Cover with plastic wrap and refrigerate for 30 minutes.

In a heavy, large skillet, heat the oil over medium-high heat. Place the crab balls in the hot oil, and mash the tops down with a fork to flatten them slightly. Fry until golden, about 5 minutes per side.

MAKES 6 SERVINGS

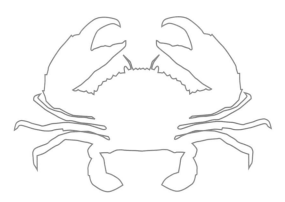

Stuffed Jalapeños Wrapped in Bacon

Everybody loves these. Make a lot of them because they'll go fast!

12 large jalapeños

12 mini hot dogs

12 little sticks of Jack cheese about half the size of the hot dogs

12 slices bacon

Prepare the grill for cooking over indirect medium heat.

Cut the tops off the jalapeños and clean out the seeds and veins with an apple corer. Stuff each jalapeño with a hot dog and a stick of cheese. Wrap the jalapeño in a slice of bacon, making sure to seal up the top. Secure with a toothpick. When all the jalapeños are stuffed and wrapped, put them in a chili grill, which is a nice tool made to cook these standing up, or put them directly on the grill. Cook until the bacon is brown and crispy, 45 minutes to 1 hour. Let cool at least 10 minutes before serving.

MAKES 12 SERVINGS

Spicy Sausage Bread

This bread goes with virtually anything and is very good served at room temperature.

8 ounces loose hot Italian sausage

¼ cup chopped green bell pepper

1 tablespoon minced red bell pepper

¼ cup finely chopped onion

1 clove garlic, minced

1 small jalapeño, minced

¼ teaspoon salt

¼ teaspoon black pepper

1 tablespoon flour

One 13.8-ounce pizza crust in a tube

1 tablespoon butter, melted

Preheat the oven to 350°F.

In a large skillet over medium-high heat, sauté the sausage, bell peppers, onion, garlic, and jalapeño until completely cooked, 8 to 10 minutes. Add the salt and pepper and mix. Remove from the skillet and drain thoroughly on paper towels.

Sprinkle the flour on a work surface, and spread out the pizza crust. Flatten the crust to 12 x 8 inches. Spread the sausage mixture evenly over the surface. Starting on a long side, roll the crust jelly-roll fashion. Place the roll on a nonstick baking sheet seam-side down. Brush with the butter.

Bake for 25 minutes, or until golden. Remove from the oven and let rest for 15 minutes. Slice into 1-inch pieces to serve.

MAKES 12 SERVINGS

Big Boy's Meatballs

Thanks to my buddy Ray Steelman for this recipe. Everybody loves Raymond's cooking.

SAUCE

2 cups prepared chili sauce

2 cups grape jelly

6 ounces beer

1 tablespoon garlic salt

1 tablespoon granulated onion

1 tablespoon dry mustard

1 teaspoon black pepper

Hot sauce

One 2-pound package prepared mini meatballs, defrosted

In a large saucepan over medium heat, combine the sauce ingredients, adding hot sauce to taste. Bring to a boil, stirring often. Add the meatballs and stir to mix well. Return to a boil, reduce to a simmer, and cook for 10 minutes, until the sauce thickens just a bit.

MAKES 8 SERVINGS

Spicy Pepperoni-Stuffed Mushrooms

These are very simple and full of flavor. You can cook them in the oven or on the grill.

1 pound white mushrooms

1 cup finely chopped pepperoni

¼ cup (1 ounce) finely grated fontina cheese (you can substitute Parmesan)

1 serrano chile, seeded and finely chopped

Preheat the oven to 350°F.

Brush the mushrooms to clean them and remove the stems, reserving them for another use. In a small bowl, combine the pepperoni, cheese, and chile and mix well. Stuff the mushrooms using a spoon and your hands. Place them on a baking sheet with the stuffing side up. When they're all stuffed, put them in the oven for 18 minutes, or until hot and bubbly. Remove to a platter and serve.

You can cook these on the grill, too. Just put them right on a grill prepared for cooking over direct medium heat, or on a piece of aluminum foil, and cook until the mushrooms are soft.

MAKES 6 TO 8 SERVINGS

Stuffed Potato Skins

These are a longtime Super Bowl tradition at my house.

6 large russet potatoes

Vegetable oil, as needed

12 slices bacon, cooked and crumbled, bacon grease reserved

1 medium green bell pepper, finely chopped

1 cup (4 ounces) shredded Cheddar cheese

2 cups sour cream

6 green onions, sliced

Preheat the oven to 350°F. Scrub the potatoes and prick them in a few places with a fork. Coat lightly with the oil. Place in the oven and cook for 1 hour, or until tender. Remove and cool completely.

Raise the oven to 450°F or prepare the grill for cooking over direct medium heat. Cut the potatoes in half lengthwise. Spoon out all but ½ inch of the pulp and save it for another use. Rub the skin sides of the potatoes with the bacon grease. You may not need it all. Fill the skins with the bacon, green pepper, and cheese, distributing them evenly among the skins.

If you're cooking them in the oven, place the skins on a baking sheet and cook for 15 minutes, or until the skins are crispy. If you're cooking on the grill, place the skins directly on the grate and cook for about 10 minutes, or until the skins are crispy. Remove from the oven or grill and top with the sour cream and then the green onions.

MAKES 12 SERVINGS

Minnesota Vikings

HOME STADIUM

Hubert H. Humphrey Metrodome
900 S. Fifth Street
Minneapolis, MN 55415

CAPACITY

64,172

OFFICIAL WEB SITE

www.vikings.com

FIRST GAME PLAYED

September 17, 1961

CHAMPIONSHIPS

NFC Champions 1969, 1973, 1974, 1976

SIGNATURE FOOD OF THE AREA

Trendy chef-based

GREAT BARBECUE

Famous Dave's

GREAT STEAKHOUSE

Manny's Steakhouse

GREAT BREW

Surly Bender

HALL OF FAMERS

Dave Casper, TE, 1983
Carl Eller, DE, 1964–1978
Jim Finks, GM, 1964–1973
Bud Grant, Coach, 1967–1983, 1985
Paul Krause, S, 1968–1979
Jim Langer, C, 1980–1981
Hugh McElhenny, RB, 1961–1962
Warren Moon, QB, 1994–1996
Alan Page, DT, 1967–1978
Jan Stenerud, PK, 1984–1985
Fran Tarkenton, QB, 1961–1966, 1972–1978
Ron Yary, OT, 1968–1981
Gary Zimmerman, OT, 1986–1992

CHEERLEADERS

Vikings Cheerleaders

BEST SEASON

1998 (15–1)

MINNEAPOLIS AND FOOD

Minneapolis is a very liberal and progressive city, both in its politics and its food culture. It's really interesting to experience just how cosmopolitan this city is while sitting right smack in the middle of "The Land of 10,000 Lakes," most of which is quite rural and the home of many sportsmen who enjoy a good fish fry or a Saturday night dinner of prime rib and a baked potato. Not that there's anything wrong with that type of meal, but Minneapolis goes way beyond that in its taste. This upscale attitude has created a vibrant dining scene driven by the talent and ambition of many high-flying local chefs, with a few celebrity chef offerings thrown in from the likes of Jean-Georges Vongerichten and Wolfgang Puck. Minneapolis is also the corporate home of Famous Dave's, the wildly successful barbecue chain, and last but not least, these are the folks who elected a professional wrestler to serve as their governor. That didn't work out so well, but you have to like them for giving it a shot.

Here are my suggestions for what to cook for a Vikings Game-Day Party. Mix and match as you wish.

Baked Brie with Chutney and Crisp Bacon (page 43)

Dr. BBQ's Grilled Shrimp Toast (page 57)

Homemade Tomato Soup (page 69)

Grilled Tuna Sandwiches with Chipotle Mayo (page 135)

Cream of Chicken Curry (page 177)

Chopped Garden Salad (page 188)

Grilled Zucchini and Yellow Squash (page 199)

Loaded Brownies (page 221)

Soups, Stews, and Chilies

I just love soups and stews and chilies, and I'm really excited about having a chapter about them here. If I wasn't a barbecue man I could happily run one of those little soup storefronts in New York City. I love to cook up different kinds, and I must say I'm pretty good at it. It seems some people just have a knack for making soup that turns out well. A friend recently told me she thought it was a nurturing thing for her; she liked to nurture the soup for the whole day. Well, I'm not exactly a nurturing kind of guy in the rest of my life, but I guess I nurture all those briskets and ribs, so it could be true about the soup too. The good news is you don't need to have been born a nurturer, because the recipes in this chapter will make your soups and stews taste just like my grandma made them.

I love to eat soups, stews, and chilies even more than I like to cook them. I rarely skip a chance to eat a cup of soup in a restaurant, and I cook them often at home. Old classics like my Grandma's Chicken Dumpling Soup (page 70) and new recipes like the Spicy Black Bean Soup (page 82) are equal favorites. Even my Championship Chili (page 98) gets made at my house on a regular basis. I guess you're getting the point here. I like soup!

There's an old story about how chili tastes better the next day. Well, let me tell you that it's true, and the same rule applies to soups and stews, so that makes them a great choice for a game-day meal. As I said earlier, I rarely skip the soup in a restaurant and I rarely skip serving a soup at a game-day party. Make it ahead and bring along the camping stove to reheat it. Styrofoam bowls will do, but big mugs are a nice touch if you don't mind taking them along. On a cold game day, there is nothing more comforting than a big hot serving of soup, stew, or chili.

Homemade Tomato Soup

This is a grown-up version of the classic but it still goes well with grilled cheese sandwiches.

¼ cup olive oil

1 medium onion, chopped

3 stalks celery, chopped

1 clove garlic, crushed

2 tablespoons all-purpose flour

2 cups vegetable stock (I use the stuff in the box)

One 28-ounce can crushed tomatoes

One 28-ounce can diced tomatoes

3 tablespoons chopped fresh basil, divided

1½ tablespoons brown sugar

1 teaspoon seasoned salt, or more as needed

½ teaspoon black pepper

In a Dutch oven or medium soup pot over medium-high heat, warm the oil. Add the onion, celery, and garlic and cook for 7 to 8 minutes, or until the onion is soft. Add the flour and mix well. Add the stock and mix well, cooking until smooth. Add both cans of tomatoes, 2 tablespoons of the basil, the sugar, 1 teaspoon salt, and pepper. Mix well. Bring to a boil, reduce to a simmer, cover, and cook for 30 minutes, stirring occasionally.

With an immersion blender or working in batches with a stand blender, puree the soup for 2 minutes or until your desired consistency. (If you like it chunky you can skip this step.) Cook for 15 minutes to rewarm. Add the remaining 1 tablespoon basil and stir. Turn off the heat and let the soup rest for 5 minutes. Stir again. Check for salt and add more if needed. You may also consider adding additional brown sugar because some canned tomatoes are more acidic than others.

MAKES 8 SERVINGS

SPECIAL FOOD-SAFETY NOTE FOR SOUPS, STEWS, AND CHILIES

Like any cooked food, soups, stews, and chilies must be kept hot until serving or quickly cooled to be reheated later. However, putting a big hot pot of liquid into the refrigerator isn't a good idea (because it heats up the other food in there) and it won't be cooled very quickly anyway. You can use the same method I use for most foods, where you distribute it into a few smaller pans with large surface areas and refrigerate until cool. Restaurants have an even better way and you can use it at home too. In the food-service world, there is a tool called an ice paddle or cooling wand, which is a heavy plastic vessel that you fill with water and freeze. When you want to cool a big pot of hot liquid, you simply drop the frozen paddle in and stir with it until the liquid is cooled. You can easily make your own smaller version of an ice paddle at home using a plastic 1- or 2-liter bottle. Wash and sanitize the bottle thoroughly, removing the label. Fill the bottle about three-quarters of the way with water and freeze it solid. Use your ice paddle to stir your soup, stew, or chili until it's cool before transferring it to refrigerator containers.

Dr. BBQ's Grandma's Chicken Dumpling Soup

This recipe was passed on from my Polish grandma to my mom, who then passed it on to my French grandma, who passed it on to me. I've been eating it my whole life, and in my mind the version I make these days is the same as it's always been, but in reality we've probably each put our own little spin on it. Either way, it's my family's favorite soup and the ultimate comfort food for me.

One 4-pound frying chicken

4 stalks celery, cut in half

1 pound carrots, peeled and cut in half

1 red onion, peeled and quartered

4 quarts water

2 cloves garlic

2 cubes chicken bouillon (I like Knorr brand)

1 teaspoon dried basil

1 teaspoon seasoned salt, or more as needed

1 teaspoon coarse ground black pepper, or more as needed

DUMPLINGS

3 cups all-purpose flour

¼ teaspoon salt

4 large eggs

¼ cup milk

Add the whole chicken, celery, carrots, and onion to an 8- to 10-quart stockpot. Pour the water over the top. If you can't fit the full 4 quarts in, just reserve the rest to add later after it cooks down. Over high heat, bring the soup to a boil and then reduce the heat to produce a slow simmer. When the scum forms on the top, scrape it off with a slotted spoon and discard. Add the garlic, bouillon, basil, 1 teaspoon salt, and 1 teaspoon pepper and stir well. Cover and simmer, stirring occasionally, for 2 hours, or until the chicken is very tender.

Carefully pour the soup through a colander into another large pot. Do this over the sink to catch any spillage. Dump the contents of the colander onto a big platter and return the soup to the stove. If you have any reserved water left, add it now.

To make the dumplings, put the flour in a large bowl and make a well in the middle. Add the salt. Crack the eggs into the well. With a big spoon, begin to beat the eggs, bringing in a little bit of flour at a time. When it gets thick, add the milk. Continue beating and bringing in the flour until it's too thick. Now you'll need to mix it with your hands the rest of the way.

Before you jump in, bring the soup to a boil and bring another medium saucepan of water to a boil right beside the soup. Use a little additional flour to coat your hands. Begin mixing the dough with your hands, bringing all of the flour from the sides of the bowl into the dough. It will remain a soft dough. When it's all well blended, start tearing off small pieces, about ½ tablespoon each, and dropping them into the soup or the water. If you drop all of the dumplings directly into the soup, it will get thick and cloudy from all the flour. If you drop all of the dumplings into the boiling water for a minute and then transfer them to the soup, you'll get a thin, clear soup. Both are good but I prefer mine somewhere in the middle, so I drop half of the dumplings directly into the soup and half into the water for a minute and then transfer them to the soup with a slotted spoon.

When all the dumplings are in the soup, cook for 30 minutes longer, stirring occasionally. Meanwhile, slice the cooked carrots and celery and set them aside. Remove all the chicken meat from the bones, discarding the skin and bones. Use a knife to cut across the grain of the big chicken pieces. After the dumplings have cooked, add the carrots, celery, and chicken meat back to the soup. Stir gently. Taste and add salt and pepper as needed.

MAKES 10 SERVINGS

New Orleans Saints

HOME STADIUM

Louisiana Superdome
1500 Poydras Street
New Orleans, LA 70112

CAPACITY

72,000

OFFICIAL WEB SITE

www.neworleanssaints.com

FIRST GAME PLAYED

September 17, 1967

CHAMPIONSHIPS

None

SIGNATURE FOOD OF THE AREA

Creole

GREAT BARBECUE

Zydeque

GREAT STEAKHOUSE

Crescent City Steak House

GREAT BREW

Abita Turbodog

HALL OF FAMERS

Doug Atkins, DE, 1967–1969
Earl Campbell, RB, 1984–1985
Jim Finks, GM, 1986–1993
Hank Stram, Coach, 1976–1977
Jim Taylor, FB, 1967

CHEERLEADERS

Saints Cheerleaders

BEST SEASON

1987 (12–3)

NEW ORLEANS AND FOOD

Maybe they call New Orleans "The Big Easy" because it's so easy to get a good meal there. There's nothing wrong with the great, old, famous places like Brennan's and Antoine's—they are among the finest restaurants in the world. But in my experience, you can get a pretty good meal just about anywhere in New Orleans and a very good one at most of the restaurants. The people in New Orleans really care about the food they eat and serve. If you ever find yourself walking around the French Quarter at midnight and you see a Lucky Dog man, you'll quickly learn that even he is into serving good food. There are so many great things about New Orleans. I love the shrimp étouffée and the filé gumbo, the crawfish and the oysters, the hurricanes and the cold beer. I love the blues and the jazz, the muffalettas and the beignets, and the blondes and the brunettes. *Laissez les bon temps rouler!*

Here are my suggestions for what to cook for a Saints Game-Day Party. Mix and match as you wish.

Sticky Fingers Cinnamon Bread (page 34)

Grilled Chili-Rubbed Shrimp Cocktail (page 56)

Dr. BBQ's Tailgate Gumbo (page 92)

High-Octane Sloppy Joes (page 112)

Shrimp Étouffée (page 168)

Loaded Cornbread Casserole (page 208)

Dried Cherry and Vanilla Bread Pudding (page 218)

¼ cup olive oil

2 pounds lean beef, cut into ½-inch cubes (I use stew meat)

1 pound carrots, sliced ½ inch thick

3 large stalks celery, sliced ½ inch thick

1 pound baby portobello mushrooms, halved and sliced ½ inch thick

1 medium onion, chopped

3 cloves garlic, minced

2 quarts water

2 cubes beef bouillon (I like Knorr brand)

1½ teaspoons salt, or more as needed

1½ teaspoons fine ground black pepper, or more as needed

1 teaspoon Gravy Master seasoning and browning sauce

1 bay leaf

½ teaspoon dried basil

½ teaspoon dried thyme

1 cup quick-cooking barley

Warm-Up Beef Barley Soup

A great way to warm up for the game.

Heat the oil in a large Dutch oven or soup kettle over medium-high heat. Add the beef, carrots, celery, portobellos, onion, and garlic. Cook for about 10 minutes, or until the onion is soft, stirring occasionally. Add the water, bouillon, 1½ teaspoons salt, 1½ teaspoons pepper, the browning sauce, bay leaf, basil, and thyme and mix well. Bring to a boil and reduce to a simmer. Cover and cook for 90 minutes, stirring occasionally. Add the barley and cook for 30 minutes longer.

Remove the bay leaf. At this time you may need to add a cup or two of additional water if the soup has cooked down too much. Check for salt and pepper and adjust as needed. Cook for an additional 30 minutes, or until the barley is tender

MAKES ABOUT 12 SERVINGS

---

10 slices thick-cut bacon

1 medium onion, finely chopped

2 cloves garlic, crushed

¼ cup all-purpose flour

One 14-ounce can vegetable broth

3 cups whole milk

1 tablespoon good-quality chili powder

1 teaspoon black pepper

1 teaspoon dry mustard

4 cups (1 pound) shredded sharp Cheddar cheese

1½ cups dried elbow macaroni, cooked

Chopped fresh parsley, for garnish

Mac and Cheese Soup

This is a unique and tasty soup that will be a favorite on those cold game days. (Pictured on page 116.)

Cut the bacon strips into quarters. In a Dutch oven over medium heat, cook the bacon until crisp. Remove it to paper towels to drain. Add a little oil to the pan if needed, then add the onion. Cook the onion for 5 minutes, stirring occasionally. Add the garlic and continue cooking until the onion is soft and lightly browned, about another 5 minutes. Add the flour and mix well. Cook for 2 minutes. Add the broth and bring to a simmer, stirring often. Add the milk, chili powder, pepper, and mustard. Return the soup to a simmer, stirring occasionally. Cook for 3 minutes. Add the cheese and bacon and continue cooking and stirring until well blended, about 4 minutes. Add the macaroni and return to a simmer. Remove from the heat and serve, sprinkling with parsley.

MAKES 8 SERVINGS

Italian Sausage Soup

Italian sausage makes everything taste good. Serve this with freshly grated Parmesan cheese and crusty bread.

1 pound bulk Italian sausage

3 tablespoons olive oil

1 medium onion, chopped

1 medium green bell pepper, chopped

1 stalk celery, chopped

1 medium yellow squash, diced

½ medium zucchini, diced

One 28-ounce can whole peeled tomatoes

One 14-ounce can vegetable broth

One 14-ounce can chicken broth

One 8½-ounce can cut green beans, drained

One 8½-ounce can kernel corn, drained

1 cup water

1 cup small shells or dried pasta of your choice

2 cloves garlic, crushed

1 teaspoon salt

1 teaspoon black pepper

1 teaspoon dried basil leaves

Crumble the sausage into a large skillet over medium heat. Sauté until the sausage is browned and cooked through. Remove the sausage to drain on a paper towel. Pour off any excess grease and return the pan to the heat. Add the oil to the skillet. Add the onion, green pepper, celery, squash, and zucchini. Cook for about 5 minutes, or until the onion is soft. Remove from the heat and set aside.

With a pair of kitchen shears, cut the tomatoes into 3 to 4 pieces each, leaving them in the can. Add the sausage, sautéed vegetables, vegetable and chicken broth, canned vegetables, water, pasta, garlic, salt, pepper, and basil to a large slow cooker. Stir to combine and cook on high for 4 to 6 hours or on low for 8 hours.

I make this soup in a slow cooker, but it works fine on the stove top, too. Just use a Dutch oven and cover and simmer it for 90 minutes, or until everything is tender. You'll need to add an additional cup or two of water as it cooks.

MAKES 10 SERVINGS

New York Giants

HOME STADIUM

Giants Stadium
East Rutherford, NJ 07073

CAPACITY

79,469

OFFICIAL WEB SITE

www.giants.com

FIRST GAME PLAYED

October 11, 1925

CHAMPIONSHIPS

NFL/NFC Champions
1933, 1934, 1935, 1938, 1939, 1941,
1944, 1946, 1956, 1958, 1959, 1961,
1962, 1963, 2000, 2007

Super Bowl Champions 1986, 1990,
2007

SIGNATURE FOOD OF THE AREA

Pizza

GREAT BARBECUE

Daisy May's

GREAT STEAKHOUSE

BLT Steak

GREAT BREW

Brooklyn Brewery

HALL OF FAMERS

Morris "Red" Badgro, E, 1930–1935
Roosevelt Brown, OT, 1953–1965
Harry Carson, LB, 1976–1988
Larry Csonka, FB, 1976–1978
Ray Flaherty, E, 1928–1929,
1931–1935
Benny Friedman, QB, 1929–1931
Frank Gifford, WR/RB, 1952–1964
Joe Guyon, RB, 1927
Mel Hein, C, 1931–1945
Wilbur "Pete" Henry, T, 1927
Arnie Herber, QB, 1944–1945
Cal Hubbard, T, 1927–1928, 1936
Sam Huff, LB, 1956–1963
Tuffy Leemans, RB, 1936–1943
Tim Mara, Owner, 1925–1959
Wellington Mara, Owner, 1959–2005
Don Maynard, WR, 1958
Hugh McElhenny, RB, 1963
Steve Owen, Coach, 1930–1953
Andy Robustelli, DE, 1956–1964
Ken Strong, RB, 1933–1935, 1939,
1944–1947
Fran Tarkenton, QB, 1967–1971
Lawrence Taylor, LB, 1981–1993
Jim Thorpe, RB, 1925
Y. A. Tittle, QB, 1961–1964
Emlen Tunnell, DB, 1948–1958
Arnie Weinmeister, DT, 1950–1953

CHEERLEADERS

None

BEST SEASON

1986 (14–2)

NEW YORK AND FOOD

I love New York. I grew up in Chicago and never went to New York because I saw no point in going to another big city on vacation. But now I go there pretty often on business and I always have a great time. New Yorkers are so passionate about their food from top to bottom. No matter where you stay, there's a little deli nearby where a guy is grinding his own coffee and getting the best bread he can find and cooking everything to order. It's really amazing how good the quality of the street food is as well. These guys all take it very seriously. There's every ethnic food you could imagine just in Manhattan, so it's impossible to identify a favorite or most popular. New Yorkers are into eating anything you can imagine, from falafel to prime beef to sea urchins. The finest cheeses and chocolates and caviar are at your fingertips. Last time I was there I enjoyed some limited-edition orange and cream M&Ms. Only in New York.

Here are my suggestions for what to cook for a Giants Game-Day Party. Mix and match as you wish.

Beer Bread with Herbs (page 36)

Spicy Pepperoni-Stuffed Mushrooms (page 64)

Manhattan Clam Chowder (page 78)

Judy's Double-Stuffed Cheeseburgers (page 139)

Tasty Salmon in a Package with Veggies (page 173)

Game-Day Caesar Salad (page 189)

Nancy P.'s Smoked Cheddar Double-Baked Potatoes (page 203)

Chocolate Chip–Mint Cookies (page 224)

Manhattan Clam Chowder

This is my favorite version of clam chowder. The sweet apple juice matches nicely with the tangy tomatoes.

4 slices bacon, diced

1 large onion, chopped

One 15-ounce can diced tomatoes

One 15-ounce can chicken broth

1 cup water

One 8-ounce can tomato sauce

1 green bell pepper, chopped

1 cup small-dice carrots

1 cup small-dice potatoes

1 cup small-dice celery

2 cloves garlic, crushed

2 teaspoons salt

½ teaspoon cayenne

2 bay leaves

2 cups minced cooked clams

½ cup apple juice

Over medium-high heat in a heavy kettle, lightly brown the bacon. Add the onion and cook until golden brown. Reduce the heat to medium-low. Add the tomatoes, broth, water, tomato sauce, bell pepper, carrots, potatoes, celery, garlic, salt, cayenne, and bay leaves. Mix well. Cover, bring to a boil, reduce the heat to a simmer, and cook for 1 hour, stirring occasionally. Add the clams and the apple juice and cook for 10 minutes more, to heat through. Remove the bay leaves to serve.

MAKES 8 SERVINGS

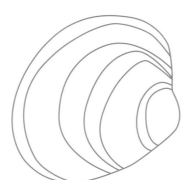

The Best Crab Soup Ever

The extravagance of crab soup with a taste of sherry is as good as it gets. Serve this one with some crusty bread on a cold day and the whole party will be warmed up.

¼ cup (2 ounces) butter

1 medium onion, finely chopped

2 stalks celery, finely chopped

1 carrot, grated

2 cloves garlic, crushed

2 tablespoons olive oil

3 tablespoons all-purpose flour

1 quart half-and-half

One 15-ounce can creamed corn

2 teaspoons salt, or more as needed

1 teaspoon sugar

1 teaspoon black pepper

1 teaspoon paprika

½ teaspoon lemon pepper

1 pound lump crabmeat, picked over

¼ cup sherry (do not use cooking sherry!)

Crusty bread, for serving

In a medium Dutch oven over medium heat, melt the butter. Add the onion, celery, carrot, and garlic and sauté for 6 to 7 minutes, until tender. Stir in the oil, and then stir in the flour. Add the half-and-half, corn, 2 teaspoons salt, sugar, the black pepper, paprika, and lemon pepper. Mix well. Bring to a simmer, stirring often, and continue to simmer for 5 minutes.

At this point I like to puree the soup with an immersion blender for 1 minute, but you can use a blender and do it in batches if you don't have one. You just want to smooth the chunks out a little, so don't blend it too long. Probably 10 to 15 seconds on a medium setting. You can also choose to leave the soup a little chunky—just make sure the vegetables are cooked enough to be soft if you're going to do that.

Add the crab and fold it in, trying not to break it up too much. Return to a simmer and cook for 2 minutes, stirring often. Turn the heat off and stir in the sherry. Check for salt and add if necessary. Serve with crusty bread.

MAKES 8 SERVINGS

Philadelphia Eagles

HOME STADIUM

NovaCare Complex
One NovaCare Way
Philadelphia, PA 19145

CAPACITY

68,400

OFFICIAL WEB SITE

www.philadelphiaeagles.com

FIRST GAME PLAYED

October 15, 1933

CHAMPIONSHIPS

NFL/NFC Champions 1948, 1949,
1960, 1980, 2004

SIGNATURE FOOD OF THE AREA

Cheese steak

GREAT BARBECUE

Pig Daddy's BBQ

GREAT STEAKHOUSE

Pat's King of Steaks

GREAT BREW

Yuengling Black & Tan

HALL OF FAMERS

Chuck Bednarik, C-LB, 1949–1962
Bert Bell, Owner, 1933–1940
Bob Brown, OT, 1964–1968
Mike Ditka, TE, 1967–1968
Bill Hewitt, E (WR), 1937–1939
Sonny Jurgensen, QB, 1957–1963
James Lofton, WR, 1993
Ollie Matson, RB, 1964–1966
Tommy McDonald, WR, 1957–1963
Art Monk, WR, 1994
Greasy Neale, Coach, 1941–1950
Pete Pihos, E (WR), 1947–1955
Jim Ringo, C, 1964–1967
Norm Van Brocklin, QB, 1958–1960
Steve Van Buren, RB, 1944–1951
Reggie White, DE, 1985–1992
Alex Wojciechowicz, LB, 1946–1950

CHEERLEADERS

Eagles Cheerleaders

BEST SEASON

2004 (13–3)

PHILADELPHIA AND FOOD

As soon as I get to Philadelphia, I go eat a cheese steak. Then I go eat a roast pork sandwich with red peppers and provolone. Only then do I begin my visit. Much like New Yorkers, the people of Philly really care about food. Just spend a couple hours on Ninth Street in the Italian Market and you'll see what I mean. The quality of the cheeses and pastas and olives and salamis and bread is unmatched anywhere. There's a game butcher and a lamb butcher and a place called the House of Pork, and they're all open to the public at the same time they're servicing the chefs of Philadelphia. If that wasn't enough, Philadelphia is also a major seaport that brings in lots of wonderful fresh seafood. There are great Italian and upscale trendy restaurants and the wonderful pretzels that are everywhere, but for me it's all about the cheese steaks. I will have an occasional pizza steak too, but it's really kind of the same thing, just dressed up a little.

Here are my suggestions for what to cook for a Eagles Game-Day Party. Mix and match as you wish.

Barbecued Chicken Nachos (page 52)

Spicy Sausage Bread (page 63)

Ray's Favorite Lamb Chili (page 95)

Cheese Steak Sandwiches (page 102)

Baked Ziti with Garlic Bread (page 183)

Grapes and Yogurt Salad (page 193)

Fresh cookies from the local Italian bakery

Spicy Black Bean Soup

This tasty and spicy soup is a vegetarian-friendly dish.

1 pound dried black beans

3 tablespoons olive oil

1 medium onion, chopped

2 stalks celery, chopped

3 cloves garlic, crushed

1 serrano chile, finely chopped

5 cups water

Two 10-ounce cans diced tomatoes with green chiles

1 cube vegetable bouillon (I like Knorr brand)

1 canned chipotle in adobo sauce, finely chopped, drained, and 1 table-spoon sauce reserved

1 teaspoon salt, or more as needed

1 teaspoon black pepper

1 teaspoon ground cumin

Chopped green onions, for garnish

Soak the beans covered with water by a couple inches, overnight in a big glass bowl. When you are ready to cook, drain the beans and set them aside.

Heat the oil in a soup pot or Dutch oven over medium heat. Add the onion, celery, garlic, and chile. Cook and stir until the onion is soft, about 5 minutes. Add the beans, water, tomatoes, bouillon cube, chipotle, reserved adobo sauce, 1 teaspoon salt, and the pepper. Bring to a boil, reduce the heat to a simmer, and cover. Cook the soup, stirring occasionally, for about 2½ hours, or until the beans are tender and the broth is creamy. Add the cumin and check for salt, adding if necessary. Serve with chopped green onions as a garnish.

MAKES 10 SERVINGS

Leftover Turkey Soup

This is a classic that everyone loves and a good way to finish up that leftover turkey. You can even make it with the leftovers from a smoked or fried turkey.

All the leftover parts, bones, skin, and meat from a cooked 18-pound turkey

1 pound carrots, peeled and quartered

1 large red onion, quartered

4 stalks celery, cut into quarters

2 large tomatoes, quartered

2 cloves garlic, sliced

2 cubes vegetable bouillon (I like Knorr brand)

1 tablespoon dried basil

1 tablespoon dried thyme

1 tablespoon seasoned salt, or more as needed

1 tablespoon black pepper

12 ounces dried curly egg noodles

Add the turkey parts and meat, carrots, onion, celery, tomatoes, garlic, bouillon, basil, thyme, 1 tablespoon salt, and pepper to a large soup pot. Cover with cold water. Over medium-high heat, bring it to a boil. Skim any scum from the top and reduce the heat to a simmer. Cover and cook for 2 hours, stirring occasionally and adding water, if needed, to keep everything covered. Pour the whole pot through a colander into another soup pot. Do this over the sink to catch any spillage. Transfer the turkey and vegetables to a baking sheet and let them cool.

Return the stock to the stove and bring it back to a boil. Add the noodles and reduce to a simmer. When you can handle the turkey, remove all the meat from the bones and set aside. Cut the carrots, celery, and onion into small pieces and add them back to the soup pot. Add the turkey meat back to the pot and stir gently. Cook until the noodles are tender. Check for salt and add if needed.

MAKES 12 SERVINGS

Smoky Beef Stew

The smokiness of the beef makes this stew delicious and well worth the effort.

2 pounds beef stew meat

1 teaspoon seasoned salt

¼ cup olive oil

1 medium onion, chopped

1 clove garlic, crushed

1 pound carrots, peeled and thickly sliced

¼ cup all-purpose flour

4 cups water

2 cubes beef bouillon (I like Knorr brand)

1½ teaspoons black pepper

1 teaspoon Gravy Master seasoning and browning sauce

4 cups peeled, cubed russet potatoes

Salt, as needed

Prepare the grill for cooking over indirect medium heat or set the smoker at 300°F, using hickory wood for flavor. Season the stew meat with the seasoned salt. Put the meat in a foil pan and grill with the lid closed or smoke for 30 minutes, tossing once. Remove from the cooker and set aside.

Heat the oil in a Dutch oven over medium-high heat. Add the onion and garlic and cook for 5 minutes, stirring often. Add the carrots and cook for 5 minutes, stirring often. Sprinkle the flour over the top and cook for 3 minutes, stirring often. Add the water, bouillon, pepper, Gravy Master, meat, and any juices that have accumulated in the foil pan. Mix well. Bring to a boil and reduce to a simmer. Cover and cook for 30 minutes, stirring occasionally. Add the potatoes and return to a simmer. Cook for 1 hour, or until the meat is tender, stirring occasionally. Check for salt and add as needed. If the stew needs thickening, remove 1 cup of the gravy and whisk it with 1 tablespoon of flour until smooth. Return to the stew and mix in. Cook for another 5 minutes and then serve.

MAKES 8 SERVINGS

Rosita's Green Chile Stew

My old buddy Scott Barrett shared this recipe with me. Scott was on my original barbecue cooking team and we have spent many days together, cooking and watching football. He's a chili-cooking champion these days and this is a home version of his award-winning green chili. Rosita is his lovely daughter and he's named it after her.

½ cup vegetable oil, as needed

2 large onions, chopped

3 pounds boneless pork loin, cut into ½-inch cubes

6 medium red potatoes, washed and diced with skin on

Four 8-ounce cans salsa verde

Two 15-ounce cans chicken broth, or more as needed

3 tablespoons ground cumin

2 tablespoons granulated garlic

1 teaspoon dried oregano

One 27-ounce can chopped green chiles, drained

One 8-ounce can diced tomatoes

Salt, as needed

Green hot sauce, as needed

In a large, heavy Dutch oven over medium-high heat, warm ¼ cup of the oil. Add the onions and cook until translucent, about 5 minutes. Transfer the onions to a bowl and set aside.

Cook the pork in the pan in 3 batches, adding oil as needed, until each batch is no longer pink, about 10 minutes per batch. When the last batch is done, drain off any grease and add all the pork back in along with the onions. Add the potatoes, salsa, broth, cumin, garlic, and oregano and mix well. Reduce to a simmer, cover and cook for 1 hour, stirring occasionally. Add the chiles and tomatoes. Mix well. Return to a simmer, cover and cook for 1 more hour, stirring occasionally and adding more broth if it gets too thick. Check for salt and add if needed. Add hot sauce as desired and stir well.

MAKES 10 SERVINGS

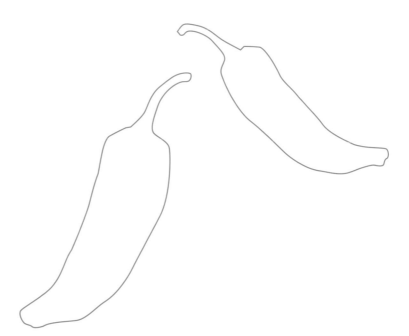

San Francisco 49ers

HOME STADIUM

Monster Park
490 Jamestown
San Francisco, CA 94124

CAPACITY

70,207

OFFICIAL WEB SITE

www.sf49ers.com

FIRST GAME PLAYED

September 17, 1950

CHAMPIONSHIPS

NFC Champions 1981, 1984, 1988, 1989, 1994

Super Bowl Champions 1981, 1984, 1988, 1989, 1994

SIGNATURE FOOD OF THE AREA

Dungeness crab

GREAT BARBECUE

Memphis Minnie's

GREAT STEAKHOUSE

Alfred's Steakhouse

GREAT BREW

Anchor Steam

HALL OF FAMERS

Fred Dean, DE, 1981–1985
Jimmy Johnson, CB, 1961–1976
John Henry Johnson, FB, 1954–1956
Ronnie Lott, S, 1981–1990
Hugh McElhenny, RB, 1952–1960
Joe Montana, QB, 1979–1992
Leo Nomellini, OT, 1950–1963
Joe Perry, RB, 1948–1960, 1963
O. J. Simpson, RB, 1978–1979
Bob St. Clair, OT, 1953–1963
Y. A. Tittle, QB, 1951–1960
Bill Walsh, Coach, 1979–1988
Dave Wilcox, LB, 1964–1974
Steve Young, QB, 1987–1999

CHEERLEADERS

Gold Rush Girls

BEST SEASON

1984 (15–1)

SAN FRANCISCO AND FOOD

San Francisco is a world-class food city. The melting pot makeup of the residents assures this, with all of the wonderful ethnic neighborhoods, anchored by their Chinatown. You can't go to San Francisco without visiting Fisherman's Wharf, where the fishing and crabbing boats are docked. You'll have great views of San Francisco Bay, the Golden Gate Bridge, and even Alcatraz while you enjoy some of the best fresh seafood in the world. The specialty in San Francisco is the Dungeness crab, and it is everywhere. The sweet meat from a Dungeness crab is possibly the best in the world and San Franciscans are proud to show it off. You'll see big pots of them cooking away and the sound of cracking shells every-where. I like to let the cooks do the work for me, but if you're ambitious they'll be happy to show you how to pick the crabs yourself. Then there's Ghirardelli Square, the legendary home of the Ghirardelli Chocolate Company, which now is home to another great group of San Francisco restaurants and nightspots. San Francisco is a beautiful city with great food everywhere.

Here are my suggestions for what to cook for a 49ers Game-Day Party. Mix and match as you wish.

Sticky Fingers Cinnamon Bread (page 34)

Crabby Crab Cakes (page 62)

The Best Crab Soup Ever (page 79)

Egg McDr. BBQ (page 101)

Game-Day Chicken and Baby Corn Stir-Fry (page 180)

Chopped Garden Salad (page 188)

Chocolate Chip–Mint Cookies (page 224)

Pozole

Pozole is a traditional Mexican stew made with pork and hominy, which is dried corn that has been treated with an alkali. Try it, you'll like it. (Pictured on page 120.)

½ cup olive oil

1 clove garlic, minced

1½ pounds boneless pork shoulder, cut into ½-inch cubes

½ cup all-purpose flour

½ cup chopped onion

One 30-ounce can yellow hominy, drained

One 15-ounce can pinto beans, drained

½ cup chopped carrots

½ cup chopped celery

½ cup chopped green chiles

2 tablespoons good-quality chili powder

4 cups chicken broth, divided

2 teaspoons dried oregano

2 teaspoons salt

½ teaspoon black pepper

½ cup sliced green onion

¼ cup chopped fresh cilantro leaves

In a large saucepan over medium heat, sauté the garlic in the oil until soft. Coat the pork with the flour, add it to the garlic oil, and brown it on all sides. Remove the pork and set it aside.

Add the onion to the pan, and cook until tender. Stir in the hominy, beans, carrots, celery, chiles, chili powder, and 2 cups of the broth. Heat everything to a boil, then reduce the heat. Cover and simmer for 15 minutes. Stir in the pork, remaining 2 cups broth, the oregano, salt, and pepper. Cover and simmer for 30 minutes, until the vegetables are tender. Just before serving, stir in the green onions and cilantro.

MAKES 8 SERVINGS

Pork and Rice Stew

A hearty stick-to-your-ribs dish that'll keep everyone warm for the whole game.

¼ cup all-purpose flour

¼ teaspoon seasoned salt, or more as needed

2 pounds pork tenderloin, trimmed and cut into bite-sized pieces

6 slices bacon

5 tablespoons olive oil, divided

1 medium green bell pepper, chopped

1 medium onion, chopped

6 medium carrots, peeled and sliced ½ inch thick

2 cloves garlic, crushed

One 14-ounce can vegetable broth

2 cups water

1 tablespoon soy sauce

1 teaspoon black pepper

½ cup uncooked long-grain white rice

Mix together the flour and ¼ teaspoon seasoned salt. In a big bowl, toss the pork with the flour mixture. In a Dutch oven over medium heat, cook the bacon until crisp. Remove the bacon to a paper towel to drain. Add 2 tablespoons of the oil. Add the meat and brown it on all sides. Remove the meat to a plate and set aside.

Add the remaining 3 tablespoons of oil to the Dutch oven. Add the bell pepper, onion, carrots, and garlic. Cook until the onions are soft. Add the broth, water, soy sauce, and pepper. Bring to a simmer. Add the meat back in. Chop the bacon and add it to the pot. Return the soup to a simmer, cover, and cook for 30 minutes, stirring occasionally. Add the rice, cover, and cook for another 30 minutes, stirring occasionally, until the rice is tender. This is meant to be a thick stew, but may need a little water for thinning at this time. Add as needed and bring back to a simmer. Check for salt and serve.

MAKES 10 SERVINGS

Seattle Seahawks

HOME STADIUM

Quest Field
800 Occidental Avenue South
Seattle, WA 98134

CAPACITY

72,000

OFFICIAL WEB SITE

www.seahawks.com

FIRST GAME PLAYED

September 12, 1976

CHAMPIONSHIPS

NFC Champions 2005

SIGNATURE FOOD OF THE AREA

Coffee

GREAT BARBECUE

Pecos Pit

GREAT STEAKHOUSE

The Metropolitan Grill

GREAT BREW

Dick's Pale Ale

HALL OF FAMERS

Carl Eller, DE, 1979
Franco Harris, RB, 1984
Steve Largent, WR, 1979–1989
Warren Moon, QB, 1997–1998

CHEERLEADERS

Sea Gals

BEST SEASON

2005 (13–3)

SEATTLE AND FOOD

Seattle has a great food scene anchored by the Pike Place Market and all the amazing fresh seafood that comes through there. The salmon is probably the favorite son of Seattle, but you'll also find oysters, clams, and crabs that people from around the world come to enjoy. The market is chock-full of little places to shop and dine, and of course you'll have to duck near the "flying fish" sign. The market's mascot is a bronze pig named Rachel, so you know these people are serious about their food. Right across the street is the original Starbucks, which is a huge tourist attraction these days, but you can still get a great cup of coffee there or at thousands of other little coffee stands in the city. Seattle is also home to many little storefronts advertising teriyaki and I love them all. They all serve pretty straight-to-the-point teriyaki chicken or beef with white rice, but it's great stuff and just doesn't need any twists. If you want twists, go to one of resident celeb-chef Tom Douglas's many restaurants. You will eat well in Seattle.

Here are my suggestions for what to cook for a Seahawks Game-Day Party. Mix and match as you wish.

Dr. BBQ's Tailgate Gumbo

I'm no Cajun, but I sure do like to eat like one and this is a great way to do that. Like in many Cajun dishes, you start here with a roux, which serves as a thickener, but if you make it dark it will add great flavor too.

STOCK

2 quarts water

One 4-pound frying chicken, cut up

2 large carrots, peeled

3 stalks celery, washed

1 medium onion, quartered

3 cloves garlic, sliced

2 cubes vegetable or chicken bouillon (I like Knorr brand)

1 tablespoon coarse ground black pepper

1 teaspoon salt

ROUX

¾ cup corn oil

¾ cup all-purpose flour

GUMBO

2 cups chopped onions

2 cups chopped celery

2 cups chopped green bell pepper

8 ounces good-quality ham, minced

6 cloves garlic, crushed

3 to 4 jalapeño chiles, chopped, seeds included

One 28-ounce can diced tomatoes

1½ tablespoons dried thyme

1 tablespoon salt, or more as needed

1 tablespoon coarse ground black pepper

1 pound small raw shrimp, peeled and deveined

4 cups white rice, hot and freshly cooked

To make the stock: Heat the water in a large Dutch oven. As the water heats, add the chicken, carrots, celery, onion, garlic, bouillon, pepper, and salt. Bring to a boil, then immediately reduce to a simmer. Cover and cook for 1 hour. Remove from the heat and let the mixture rest at room temperature for another hour. Pour the mixture through a colander into a large heatproof bowl or pot. Do this over a sink, to catch any spillage. Reserve the vegetables for another use, or have them for a snack. Let the chicken cool and remove the skin and bones, keeping the chicken in large chunks. Reserve the stock.

To make the roux: Preheat a clean, large Dutch oven over medium heat. Add the oil and flour. Cook, stirring constantly with a wooden spoon, until the roux is a dark brown chocolate color. This will take a long time and can't be rushed. (I timed one recently and it took almost an hour.) Be very careful not to burn the roux, or you'll need to start all over. Turn the heat down if you need to. This is particularly high-risk toward the end. As soon as you think the roux is dark enough, or your nerve runs out, add the onions, celery, and bell pepper for the gumbo and continue stirring. This will cool the roux and end the risk of it burning.

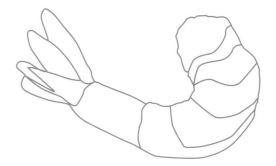

For the gumbo: Cook and stir for 5 minutes, until the vegetables get soft. Add the ham, garlic, and jalapeños. Continue cooking and stirring for another 5 minutes. Add the canned tomatoes with their juice. Return to a simmer and cook for another 5 minutes. Add 2 quarts of the reserved stock, the thyme, 1 tablespoon salt, and the pepper. Bring to a boil, reduce the heat, and simmer on low for 1¾ hours, adding more stock as needed. If the stock runs out, just add water. The consistency should be a thick soup. Add the reserved chicken and the shrimp and return the gumbo to a simmer, stirring occasionally. Cook for about 10 minutes, or until the shrimp are pink. Check for salt and place a pile of rice along the side of the bowl before adding the gumbo.

MAKES 12 SERVINGS

NOTE

If you're cooking this ahead to take to the game, stop the recipe right before the shrimp go in. Shrimp cook quickly and get rubbery if over-cooked. Add the chicken alone and cool the gumbo quickly (see page 69), then refrigerate it overnight. At the game, bring the gumbo back to a simmer and then add the shrimp. You should bring along any leftover stock too, as you may need it to thin the gumbo.

Big Pot Tailgate Chili

This is the recipe for a big party of hungry chiliheads. It's pretty spicy, so use a few less jalapeños if you want it mild or a few more if you dare. Notice the chocolate in there? It's actually a popular ingredient in chili, especially in the Cincinnati style. Serve with grated cheese and oyster crackers.

1 pound bacon

3 large onions, chopped

4 large green bell peppers, chopped

4 stalks celery, chopped

6 cloves garlic, chopped

5 pounds ground chuck

Three 28-ounce cans diced tomatoes

Four 15-ounce cans beef broth

1 cup pickled sliced jalapeños (from the jar), drained

¾ cup good-quality chili powder

½ cup packed brown sugar

½ cup chocolate chips

¼ cup ground cumin

2 tablespoons black pepper

1 tablespoon salt

Three 15-ounce cans dark kidney beans, drained

Three 15-ounce cans pinto beans, drained

In a large soup pot over medium heat, cook the bacon until crisp. Remove the bacon to drain on paper towels. Add the onions, bell peppers, celery, and garlic and mix well. Continue cooking, stirring often, for about 15 minutes, or until everything is soft.

In a separate Dutch oven or pot over medium-high heat, brown one-third of the meat. When the meat is browned, add it to the vegetable pot and repeat with the other two-thirds of the meat. Add the tomatoes and continue cooking for 5 minutes. Add the broth and bring the soup to a boil, stirring often. Reduce the heat to a simmer and continue stirring. Chop the bacon and add it to the pot along with the jalapeños, chili powder, sugar, chocolate chips, cumin, pepper, and 1 tablespoon salt. Mix well. Add the beans and mix well. Return to a simmer. Cover and cook for 1 hour. Remove the cover and cook for 1 more hour, until the flavors are combined. Check for salt and add if needed.

MAKES 25 SERVINGS

Ray's Favorite Lamb Chili

Lamb chili is my personal favorite. I think the rich flavor and mouthfeel of lamb make a great combo with the strong flavors of chili.

1 teaspoon salt, or more as needed

1 tablespoon plus 1 teaspoon black pepper

2 tablespoons all-purpose flour

3 pounds lean lamb meat, cut into ½-inch cubes

7 slices bacon

½ cup vegetable oil, divided

1 large yellow onion, chopped

3 stalks celery, chopped

2 green bell peppers, chopped

2 jalapeños, finely chopped, seeds and all

4 cloves garlic, crushed

Two 14½-ounce cans diced tomatoes with green chiles

One 14-ounce can vegetable broth

One 14-ounce can beef broth

½ cup good-quality chili powder

2 tablespoons ground cumin

1 tablespoon dried oregano

Two 15½-ounce cans dark red kidney beans, drained

In a small bowl, combine 1 teaspoon salt, 1 teaspoon of the black pepper, and the flour. Mix well. Put the meat in a large bowl and sprinkle the flour mixture over it. Toss well until the meat is evenly coated and then set aside.

Heat a stockpot or Dutch oven over medium heat. Add the bacon and cook until crisp. Remove the bacon to paper towels to drain. Add ¼ cup of the oil. Add the onion, celery, bell peppers, jalapeños, and garlic. Cook and stir for 8 minutes, or until the onion is soft. Remove the vegetables to a bowl. Add the remaining ¼ cup oil to the pot. Add the meat and cook, stirring occasionally, for 10 minutes, or until it is well browned. Add the vegetable mixture back in. Add the tomatoes, both broths, the chili powder, cumin, 1 tablespoon black pepper, and the oregano. Mix well. Crumble the bacon and add it to the pot. Bring to a simmer. Cover and cook for 1 hour, stirring occasionally, or until the lamb is tender. Add 1 cup of water if the chili gets too thick. Add the beans, stir well, and cook for another 20 minutes to heat them through. Check for salt and add if needed.

MAKES 8 SERVINGS

St. Louis Rams

1937–1942, 1944–1945 Cleveland Rams, 1946–1994 Los Angeles Rams, 1995–present St. Louis Rams

HOME STADIUM

Edward Jones Dome
701 Convention Plaza
St. Louis, MO 63101

CAPACITY

70,000

OFFICIAL WEB SITE

www.stlouisrams.com

FIRST GAME PLAYED

September 10, 1937

CHAMPIONSHIPS

NFC Champions 1950, 1951, 1979, 1999, 2001

WFC Champions 1955

NFL Champions 1945, 1951

Super Bowl Champions 1999

SIGNATURE FOOD OF THE AREA

Toasted ravioli

GREAT BARBECUE

Super Smokers

GREAT STEAKHOUSE

Dierdorf & Hart's Steak House

GREAT BREW

Michelob Amber Bock

HALL OF FAMERS

George Allen, Coach, 1966–1970

Eric Dickerson, RB, 1983–1987

Tom Fears, E, 1948–1956

Elroy "Crazy Legs" Hirsch, HB, 1949–1957

David "Deacon" Jones, DE, 1961–1971

Tom Mack, OG, 1966–1978

Ollie Matson, HB, 1959–1962

Merlin Olsen, DT, 1962–1976

Dan Reeves, Owner-Administrator, 1941–1971

Jackie Slater, T, 1976–1995

Norm Van Brocklin, QB, 1949–1957

Bob Waterfield, QB, 1945–1952

Jack Youngblood, DE, 1971–1984

CHEERLEADERS

St. Louis Rams Cheerleaders

BEST SEASON

2001 (14–2)

ST. LOUIS AND FOOD

The most famous of all food in St. Louis is without a doubt the Italian food served in the neighborhood known as "The Hill." It's a very busy and very authentic old Italian neighborhood and it's frequented by locals and tourists alike. You'll find wonderful old restaurants, bakeries, and gelato stands that have all the character of the homeland. It's like going back in time and I hope it never changes. The one dish that's served everywhere is the toasted ravioli. It's just a good-quality ravioli lightly breaded and fried, served with a marinara dipping sauce. It's great stuff, but it's definitely not toasted. No matter, be sure to order some when you're there. My other favorite food stop in St. Louis is Ted Drewes for the best frozen custard on the planet. I'll usually join my friend Mike and his family for an evening of eating Ted Drewes custard, playing checkers, and watching TV when I'm in St. Louis. I'll have a pint of the chocolate chip, please.

Here are my suggestions for what to cook for a Rams Game-Day Party. Mix and match as you wish.

Spicy Sausage Bread (page 63)

Spicy Pepperoni-Stuffed Mushrooms (page 64)

Italian Sausage Soup (page 75)

Judy's Double-Stuffed Cheeseburgers (page 139)

Baked Ziti with Garlic Bread (page 183)

Game-Day Caesar Salad (page 189)

Homemade cannoli from a bakery on The Hill

¼ cup vegetable oil

3½ pounds trimmed tri-tip, cut into ⅜-inch cubes

1 cup water

1 cube beef bouillon (I like Knorr brand)

FIRST DUMP

Half a 10½-ounce can Campbell's beef consommé

Half an 8-ounce can tomato sauce

¼ cup good-quality chili powder

One small envelope Sazón Goya sin Achiote

2 tablespoons granulated onion

1 tablespoon granulated garlic

1 tablespoon ground cumin

1 teaspoon salt

¼ teaspoon ground jalapeño (powder)

SECOND DUMP

2 tablespoons good-quality chili powder

Water as needed

THIRD DUMP

The rest of the canned tomato sauce

The rest of the canned consommé

2 tablespoons good-quality chili powder

1 cube chicken bouillon

Pinch of salt, as needed

Pinch of brown sugar, as needed

Pinch of jalapeño powder, as needed

Dr. BBQ's Championship Chili

This really is my cook-off chili recipe. I've done pretty well with it, even grabbing the Wisconsin State Championship in 2001. The traditional way to cook contest chili is to add the spices in layers, also known as "dumps." The cooks usually have these dumps made up ahead of time and each in its own zip-top bag. My chili powder of choice is San Antonio Red from Pendery's in Dallas. I also buy my granulated onion, granulated garlic, and ground cumin from them. It's all super fresh and great stuff. You can find them on the Web at www.penderys.com. When cooking in a chili cook-off, don't be afraid to go a little heavy on the salt. It's an old trick for judges with burned-out tastebuds. Don't ever add beer, black pepper, or green bell pepper, though, because the judges typically don't like those flavors for competition chili.

In a Dutch oven over medium-high heat, warm the oil. Add the tri-tip and cook for 10 minutes, stirring occasionally, until browned. Add the water and bouillon. Bring to a boil, reduce the heat to a simmer, and cook for 30 minutes.

Add the first dump. Cover and simmer for about another 20 minutes. Stir well and remove from the heat. Let rest at room temperature for 1 hour.

About 45 minutes before turn-in (or whenever you want to serve it), bring the chili back to a simmer, then add the second dump. Simmer for 20 minutes. Add the third dump. Simmer for 10 minutes. Check the consistency and add a little water if needed or turn up the heat and cook it down a little. When the consistency is good, check for salt, brown sugar, and jalapeño powder and add as needed.

Cook the chili consistency to your preference. Add water as you go and judge the doneness of the meat as you go. The tri-tip has a big window of good texture without getting mushy.

MAKES 8 SERVINGS

½ cup olive oil

1 large onion, chopped

1 large red bell pepper, chopped

4 medium carrots, chopped

3 cloves garlic, minced

¼ cup plain dried bread crumbs

3 canned chipotles in adobo sauce, drained and finely chopped

3 tablespoons ground cumin

2 tablespoons good-quality chili powder

1 teaspoon paprika

One 15-ounce can tomato sauce

One 14½-ounce can diced tomatoes

½ cup pearl barley, cooked

One 15-ounce can black beans, drained

One 15-ounce can chili beans

1 cup water

1 tablespoon brown sugar

2 teaspoons salt

Bean and Barley Vegetarian Chili

You won't miss the meat at all in this hearty chili.

In a large soup pot over medium heat, warm the oil. Sauté the onion, bell pepper, carrots, and garlic for 6 to 8 minutes, or until tender. Reduce the heat to medium-low, and stir in the bread crumbs, chipotles, cumin, chili powder, and paprika. Combine thoroughly. Add the tomato sauce, diced tomatoes, and barley. Stir. Add the black beans, chili beans, water, brown sugar, and salt. Mix well. Reduce the heat to low, cover, and simmer for 30 minutes, stirring occasionally, until the flavors come together.

MAKES 8 SERVINGS

---

1 tablespoon vegetable oil

1 large onion, chopped

1 large green bell pepper, chopped

4 cloves garlic, crushed

One 28-ounce can diced tomatoes

2 cups water, or more as needed

One 10½-ounce can beef consommé

4 canned chipotles in adobo sauce, chopped

¼ cup plus 1 tablespoon good-quality chili powder

1 tablespoon ground cumin

½ teaspoon salt

2 pounds grilled or smoked beef chuck or sirloin, diced

One 15-ounce can kidney beans, drained

Game-Day Smoky Chili

A black cast-iron kettle specialty.

In a Dutch oven over medium heat, warm the oil. Add the onion and bell pepper and cook until soft. Add the garlic and cook a few more minutes. Add the tomatoes, 2 cups water, the consommé, chipotles, chili powder, cumin, and salt. Mix in well and bring to a simmer. Add the beef and return the chili to a simmer. Cook for 1 hour. Add the beans and more water, if needed. Cook another 30 minutes, until desired thickness.

MAKES 8 SERVINGS

NOTE

These chili recipes can be doubled for a bigger crowd.

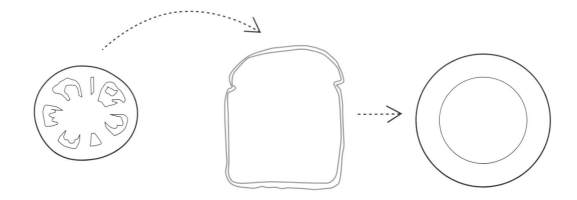

Great Sandwiches

Great sandwiches always have a place at a game-day meal. I can't help but think that the Earl of Sandwich was watching some early version of NFL football when he came up with the idea. Now this is just a guess, but I'm thinking there was a football-shaped rock or something that was found and some guys were throwing it around and there might have been a random tree shaped like a goalpost and an incline where the fans could sit and watch the new game come to life. So maybe the Earl of Sandwich was there, and when his servants brought him his lunch of a big piece of grilled oxen and some sliced onion and tomato along with an early version of an onion roll, someone had the great idea to layer it all, and the roast beef sandwich was born. They probably didn't have any mayo, but that was before the beef got to be so lean, so it was OK.

Since then, the sandwich has evolved to be a big part of every culture's cuisine. From pita-stuffed pocket bread to a grilled hamburger, we all like sandwiches and they're perfect for game day. A sandwich just fits in with watching the game because you don't need utensils and you can hold it in one hand and a beverage in the other hand, or you can set your beverage down and use that spare hand for emphasizing your point in the discussion over whether the receiver actually stayed in bounds (this will help your team) or gesturing to the ref about how bad you think his call was (this will *not* help your team). The sandwich is also the perfect food to be eaten while standing up, and those of us who have our game-day party in the parking lot appreciate that.

I like to serve sandwiches displayed on a platter and cut into halves or even quarters so the lighter eaters can still sample everything. Don't worry about the big eaters—they'll grab a couple of pieces. If there is a sauce or dressing that some may not like, be sure to make a few sandwiches without it or just serve the sauce on the side for all to use as they wish, and everyone will be happy.

Egg McDr. BBQ

These are great for those early-morning game-day meals.

6 thin boneless pork chops

Your favorite barbecue rub, as needed

6 English muffins

6 large eggs

6 slices pepper Jack cheese

Prepare the grill (or a grill pan) for cooking over direct high heat. Season the pork chops lightly with the barbecue rub and grill them hot and fast until cooked through, about 2 minutes per side. Remove them to a platter and set aside.

Toast the English muffins and set aside. Fry the eggs over medium heat, sort of like over easy but breaking the yolks just before flipping. I like to cook them lightly so the yolks are still a little runny, but you can cook them hard if you like. Place a pork chop, an egg, and a slice of cheese on each of 6 muffin halves. Top with the other muffin halves and serve.

MAKES 6 SANDWICHES

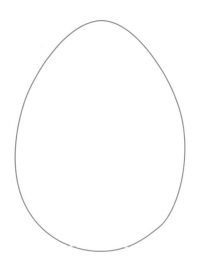

Fresh Breakfast Burritos

These are flavorful and good and can easily be made at the game or made ahead, individually wrapped in foil, and warmed up quickly on the grill.

6 thick slices bacon, diced

1 cup finely chopped onion

1 cup finely chopped green bell pepper

1 cup finely diced tomato

1 jalapeño, minced

½ teaspoon black pepper

¼ teaspoon salt

1 tablespoon butter

12 large eggs, lightly beaten

Six 10-inch flour tortillas, warmed

1 tablespoon hot sauce (optional)

1 cup (4 ounces) shredded Jack cheese

Salsa, for serving

In a large skillet over medium heat, begin cooking the bacon. When the bacon begins to render some fat, add the onion and bell pepper. Cook for 3 minutes. Add the tomato, jalapeño, black pepper, and salt and continue cooking, stirring occasionally, until the bacon is crisp. Add the butter and mix it in. Add the eggs and mix well. Cook, stirring often, just until the eggs are set, and then quickly remove them from the heat.

Divide the egg mixture among the tortillas. Top each with some hot sauce (if using) and some cheese. Roll each burrito up, packing the filling tightly and tucking in the sides, trying to get it all sealed up. Set the burritos on a plate with the seam-sides down and let them rest for a couple of minutes to seal. Serve with salsa if desired.

MAKES 6 BURRITOS

Cheese Steak Sandwiches

This is very similar to what you'll get at a real steak joint in South Philly. You can get mushrooms and peppers at many of these places, but I've never actually seen a local order one that way. (I think that stuff is for the tourists.) They do sometimes order a pizza steak, which includes a little tomato sauce and provolone cheese instead of the Cheez Whiz, but this is by far the most popular version.

½ cup vegetable oil, divided

2 medium onions, chopped

2 pounds top round, sliced paper-thin

2 tablespoons seasoned salt

6 hoagie rolls

1½ cups Cheez Whiz

In a large skillet over medium-high heat, warm half of the oil. Add the onions and cook, stirring occasionally, until they are soft. Season the meat with the seasoned salt. Set it aside.

In another large skillet over high heat, warm the remaining ¼ cup of the oil. Add the meat and cook it for about 10 minutes, to medium doneness. Spread the Cheez Whiz on the hoagie rolls. Divide the meat among them and top with the onions.

MAKES 6 SANDWICHES

Italian Beef Sandwiches

In Chicago, this is the food of the neighborhoods. Yeah, we eat plenty of hot dogs too, but Italian beef is the most popular sandwich in the Windy City.

RUB

1 teaspoon salt

1 teaspoon black pepper

1 teaspoon granulated garlic

One 4-pound sirloin tip or bottom round roast

GRAVY

1¼ cups water

¼ cup olive oil

3 cloves garlic, crushed

1 tablespoon dried oregano

2 teaspoons salt

1 teaspoon dried basil

1 teaspoon red pepper flakes

1 teaspoon black pepper

10 crusty French rolls

Chicago-Style Sweet Peppers (facing page)

Giardiniera, as needed (available at most grocery stores, near the pickles)

Preheat the oven to 450°F. Combine the rub ingredients and sprinkle them all over the roast. Place the roast on a rack in a small roasting pan, and roast for 30 minutes.

Meanwhile, combine the gravy ingredients in a medium bowl and mix well. After 30 minutes, turn the oven down to 350°F. Remove the roasting pan from the oven. Slowly pour the gravy into the bottom of the pan. Cover and return it to the oven for 1 hour and 15 minutes, or until the meat reaches an internal temperature of 150°F. Remove it from the oven, uncover, and let cool for 30 minutes. Wrap the roast in foil and refrigerate it for at least 4 hours but preferably overnight. Transfer the gravy to a heatproof measuring cup, being sure to get any stuck stuff from the bottom of the pan. At this point you should have 2 cups of gravy. If you're short, add enough water to make 2 cups. Cover and refrigerate with the beef.

The next day, take the meat out of the refrigerator and slice it as thinly as possible. Slicing it while cold will help. This is a very important part of the recipe. If you can use an electric slicer, that would be the best, as you want it very thin. If not, get your best sharp knife and take your time slicing it as thinly as you possibly can. The authentic Chicago Italian beef is sliced paper thin and that is key to its taste.

Now preheat the oven to 350°F. Add the beef and the gravy to a roasting pan or an oven-safe Dutch oven. Toss well to coat all of the beef with gravy. Cover and cook in the oven for 20 minutes. Uncover and toss the meat to coat again. Cover and cook for another 20 minutes. Layer the meat on crusty French rolls with Chicago-Style Sweet Peppers and spicy hot giardiniera.

MAKES 10 SANDWICHES

Chicago-Style Sweet Peppers

This one is pretty simple, but it's the perfect complement to the Italian beef.

¼ cup olive oil

2 green bell peppers, thickly sliced from top to bottom (not in rings)

1 red bell pepper, thickly sliced from top to bottom (not in rings)

Heat the oil in a skillet over medium heat. Add the peppers and cook for about 5 minutes, or just until soft. Transfer the peppers and oil to a bowl and serve at room temperature with the beef.

MAKES 2 CUPS

Tampa Bay Buccaneers

HOME STADIUM

Raymond James Stadium
4201 North Dale Mabry Highway
Tampa, FL 33607

CAPACITY

65,657

OFFICIAL WEB SITE

www.buccaneers.com

FIRST GAME PLAYED

September 12, 1976

CHAMPIONSHIPS

NFC Champions 2002
Super Bowl Champions 2002

SIGNATURE FOOD OF THE AREA

Cuban

GREAT BARBECUE

Jimbo's

GREAT STEAKHOUSE

Bern's

GREAT BREW

Ybor City Brewing Company

HALL OF FAMERS

Lee Roy Selmon, LB, 1976–1984
Steve Young, QB, 1985–1986

CHEERLEADERS

Buccaneers Cheerleaders

BEST SEASON

2002 (12–4)

TAMPA AND FOOD

I live 45 minutes from Tampa these days, so it's my adopted big city now and I love it here. I travel a lot during the summer and get to stay close to home during the winter, and I have to tell you that the winter weather in Tampa is perfect. There are three major influences on the food in Tampa. The legendary Cuban history of the area is still strong, and there are some great Cuban restaurants all over town and many great Cuban families carrying on the tradition. The best whole hog I've ever eaten was cooked in the Cuban style at a home in Tampa. Many thanks to the Lopez family! But Florida is also part of the South, and as soon as you get away from the trendy coastal areas you'll find plenty of down-home country cooking, with collard greens and grits as the staples of life. Then you add the wonderful fresh seafood from Tampa Bay and the Gulf of Mexico and you've got three great food traditions colliding in Tampa, and we're all pretty happy about it.

Here are my suggestions for what to cook for a Buccaneers Game-Day Party. Mix and match as you wish.

Grilled Chili-Rubbed Shrimp Cocktail (page 56)

Grilled Mahi Mahi Skewers with Peppered Bacon (page 59)

Spicy Black Bean Soup (page 82)

BCT Sandwiches (page 141)

Chipotle Chicken Tacos (page 133)

"Just Can It" Bean Salad (page 198)

Grilled Grits (page 208)

Citrus Flan (page 226)

Barbecued Pulled Pork Sandwiches

This is what real barbecue is all about. A slow-cooked pork shoulder is as good as it gets. Yes, the "butt" actually comes from the shoulder. It's the shoulder blade or the "butt" end of the whole shoulder. These sandwiches are best served topped with coleslaw. Pick one of mine or use your family favorite. (Pictured on page 119.)

RUB

3 tablespoons salt

2 tablespoons black pepper

1 tablespoon granulated garlic

1 tablespoon paprika

One 7- to 8-pound pork butt, fat cap trimmed off

2 tablespoons vegetable oil

½ cup apple juice

2 cups Dr. BBQ's Carolina Barbecue Sauce (facing page)

12 hamburger buns

Coleslaw, as needed

To make the rub, in a small bowl, combine the salt, pepper, granulated garlic, and paprika. Rub the meat with the oil and then sprinkle it liberally with the rub. Put it in the refrigerator for at least 30 minutes and up to 12 hours.

Prepare the grill or smoker for cooking over indirect low (275°F) heat, using hickory and cherry wood for flavor. Put the butt in the cooker and cook until the internal temperature is 160°F. This should take 6 to 8 hours, depending on your cooker.

Lay out a big double piece of heavy-duty aluminum foil and put the pork butt in the middle. As you begin to close up the package, pour the apple juice over the top of the butt and then seal the package, taking care not to puncture it. Put it back in the cooker. Return the package to the cooker and cook until the meat reaches an internal temperature of 195°F. This should take another 2 to 3 hours. Remove the package from the cooker to a baking sheet. Open the top of the foil to let the steam out and let it rest for 30 minutes. Using heavy neoprene gloves or a pair of tongs and a fork, transfer the meat to a big pan. It will be very tender and hard to handle. Discard the juices, as they will be quite fatty. Shred the meat, discarding the fat and bones. It should just fall apart. Continue to pull the meat until it's shredded enough to make a sandwich. Add 1 cup of the sauce and mix well. Reserve the additional sauce for serving on the side. Serve the barbecue on fluffy white buns topped with coleslaw.

MAKES 12 SANDWICHES

Barbecued Brisket Sandwiches

Just like you'll get in a real barbecue joint in Texas or Kansas City.

One 5- to 6-pound brisket flat with the fat cap left on

Your favorite barbecue rub

1 cup beef broth

2 cups of your favorite barbecue sauce

12 hamburger buns

1 large onion, thinly sliced

Dill pickle chips

Pickled sliced jalapeños (from the jar)

At least a couple of hours and up to 8 hours before you plan to start cooking, season the brisket heavily with the barbecue rub. Wrap it in plastic and return it to the refrigerator.

Prepare the grill or smoker for cooking over indirect low (275°F) heat, using pecan or hickory wood for flavor. Cook the brisket fat-side down for 1 hour and then flip it to fat-side up. Cook until it reaches an internal temperature of 160°F. This should take 3 to 4 hours total, depending on your cooker.

Lay out a big double layer of heavy-duty aluminum foil. Lay the brisket on the foil fat-side up. As you bring up the sides of the foil, add the broth. Wrap the foil up around the brisket, sealing it tightly, and return it to the cooker. After another hour, begin checking the internal temperature. When it reaches 195°F, take it out. This should take 1 to 3 more hours, depending on your cooker. Let the brisket rest for 1 hour, wrapped.

Unwrap the brisket, being careful of the hot liquid in the foil. Save the liquid and skim the fat from the top. Mix 1 cup of the cooking liquid (discarding the rest) with the barbecue sauce. Slice the brisket thinly against the grain and serve, or cool and slice it the next day. Serve the brisket on the buns with the sauce, onion, pickles, and jalapeños offered as condiments.

MAKES 12 SANDWICHES

Dr. BBQ's Carolina Barbecue Sauce

1 cup cider vinegar

2/3 cup ketchup

2 teaspoons sugar

1 teaspoon salt

1 teaspoon Worcestershire sauce

1/2 teaspoon red pepper flakes

In a small saucepan, mix together the vinegar, ketchup, sugar, salt, Worcestershire, and pepper flakes. Cook over low heat for 5 minutes, stirring to blend.

MAKES ABOUT 2 CUPS

Barbecued Bologna Sandwiches

This simple dish is a delicacy in the South. I like to serve it on hamburger buns topped with coleslaw and barbecue sauce. Then just cut the sandwiches into halves or quarters to serve.

One 3-pound chub bologna
(if you can't find a 3-pound chub, just ask for an unsliced chunk at the deli)

¼ cup black pepper

Your favorite barbecue sauce, as needed

12 hamburger buns

Creamy Coleslaw (page 195)

Prepare the grill or smoker for cooking over indirect low (250°F) heat, using apple wood chips for flavor. Cut a series of ¼-inch-deep slits all over the bologna. I just do a diamond pattern, but if you're the artistic type, get creative. As it cooks, the bologna will shrink and the design will become visible. Now sprinkle the black pepper all over the bologna. Put the bologna on the grill or smoker and cook until it reaches an internal temperature of 160°F. This should take 2 to 3 hours, depending on your cooker.

Remove the bologna from the grill and immediately brush it with barbecue sauce. If it gets done early, just wrap it in foil and let it rest in a warm place until serving time. When it's time to serve, cut 12 thick slices and put each one on a bun bottom. Top with Creamy Coleslaw, barbecue sauce, and the bun tops.

MAKES 12 SANDWICHES

Steak Sandwiches on Garlic Bread with Grilled Onions

Any game-day crowd will be happy to have you serve these.

3 tablespoons olive oil

1 large onion, halved and thinly sliced

½ cup (4 ounces) unsalted butter, at room temperature

1½ teaspoons granulated garlic

6 large kaiser rolls, split

6 thinly sliced rib-eye steaks

Your favorite barbecue rub

In a medium skillet over medium-high heat, warm the oil. Add the onion and cook until golden brown, about 10 minutes. Transfer to a bowl and set aside.

In a small bowl, mix the butter with the garlic. Spread the garlic butter evenly on all the rolls. (This can all be done the day ahead.) Prepare the grill for cooking over direct high heat. Season the steaks on both sides with the rub. Grill the rolls butter-side down quickly until golden brown. Transfer them to a platter. Grill the steaks for 3 to 4 minutes per side, or until medium-rare. Place each steak on a roll and top with the grilled onion. You can cut the sandwiches in half for a big crowd.

MAKES 6 SANDWICHES

High-Octane Sloppy Joes

This is a recipe I've been meaning to write for a long time. I think it was worth the wait. These are best served in a bowl with a spoon.

3 tablespoons vegetable oil

1 small yellow onion, finely chopped

1 poblano chile, seeded and finely chopped

1 serrano chile, seeded and finely chopped

1 jalapeño chile, seeded and finely chopped

3 cloves garlic, crushed

½ teaspoon crushed fresh ginger

2 pounds ground chuck

2 cups water

1 cup prepared chili sauce

One 6-ounce can tomato paste

1 tablespoon good-quality chili powder

1½ teaspoons dry mustard

1½ teaspoons salt

1½ teaspoons black pepper

12 hamburger buns

2 cups (8 ounces) shredded sharp Cheddar cheese

Heat the oil in a medium skillet over medium heat. Add the onion, chiles, garlic, and ginger and cook, stirring occasionally, for about 7 minutes, or until the onion is soft. Meanwhile, heat a Dutch oven over medium-high heat and add the ground chuck. Brown the chuck, breaking it up as much as possible as it cooks. When the meat is fully cooked, add the onion mixture, water, chili sauce, tomato paste, chili powder, mustard, salt, and pepper. Mix well and bring to a simmer. Cover and cook for 30 minutes, stirring occasionally, until thickened.

Place the bottoms of the buns in bowls, and divide the sloppy joe mixture evenly among the buns. Top with the shredded cheese. Replace the tops of the buns and serve with a spoon.

MAKES 12 SERVINGS

CATFISH TACOS WITH CITRUS SALSA
(RECIPE ON PAGE 134)

BLOODY MARY CHICKEN WINGS

(RECIPE ON PAGE 46)

THE BLOODY DOCTOR

(RECIPE ON PAGE 232)

MAC AND CHEESE SOUP

(RECIPE ON PAGE 74)

BUFFALO CHICKEN BREAST SANDWICHES
(RECIPE ON PAGE 141)

GRILLED SIRLOIN STEAK WITH TWO-MUSHROOM SAUTÉ
(RECIPE ON PAGE 166)

BARBECUED PULLED PORK SANDWICHES
(RECIPE ON PAGE 108)

POZOLE

(RECIPE ON PAGE 88)

PEACHY BABY BACK RIBS
(RECIPE ON PAGE 154)

DR. BBQ'S LOBSTER WITH
CHILI-LIME BUTTER
(RECIPE ON PAGE 169)

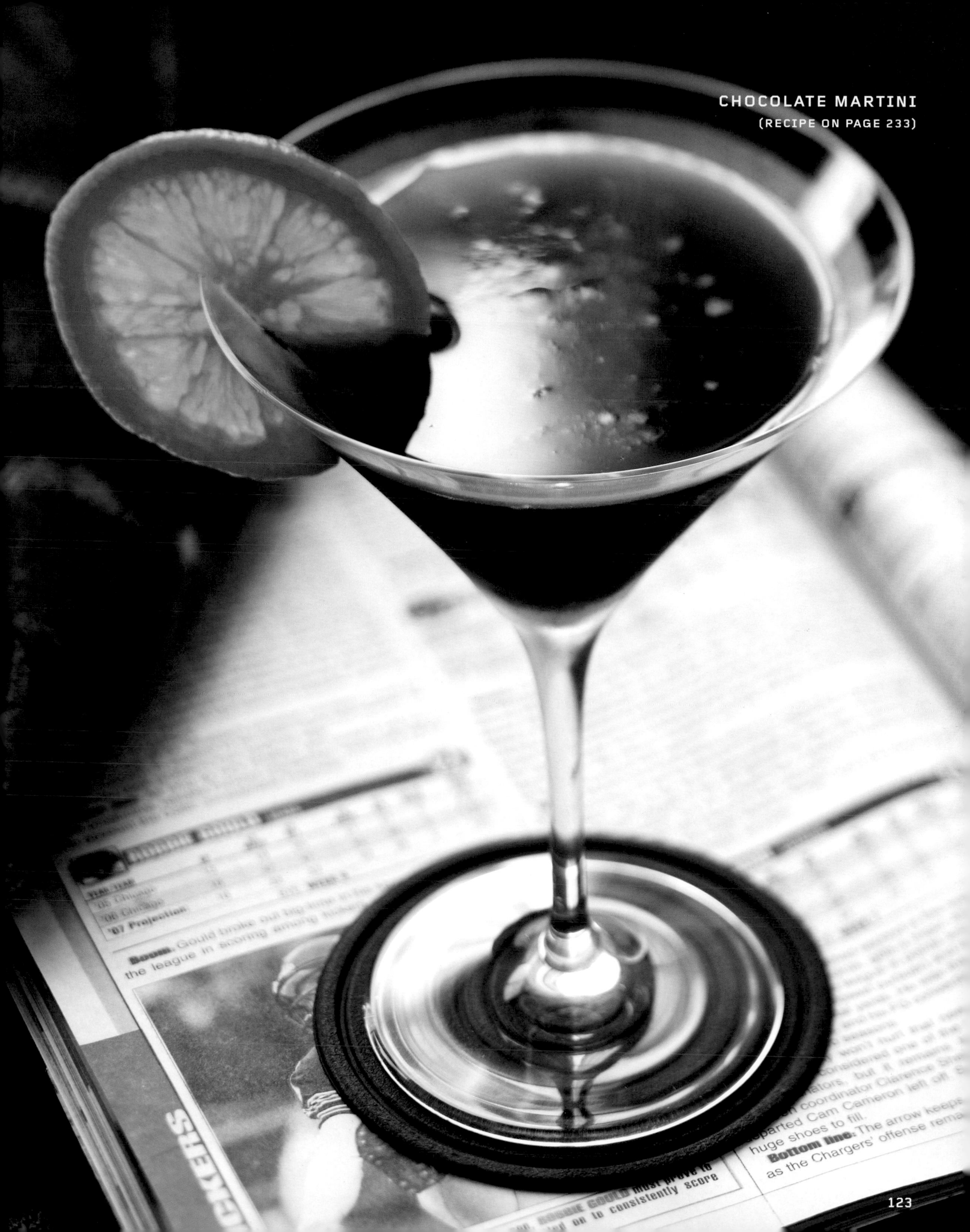

CHOCOLATE MARTINI

(RECIPE ON PAGE 233)

STICKY FINGERS CINNAMON BREAD
(RECIPE ON PAGE 34)

DOENEE'S NUTELLA BARS
(RECIPE ON PAGE 219)

BBQ-RUBBED FRUIT KABOBS

(RECIPE ON PAGE 206)

NANCY P.'S SMOKED CHEDDAR DOUBLE-BAKED POTATOES
(RECIPE ON PAGE 203)

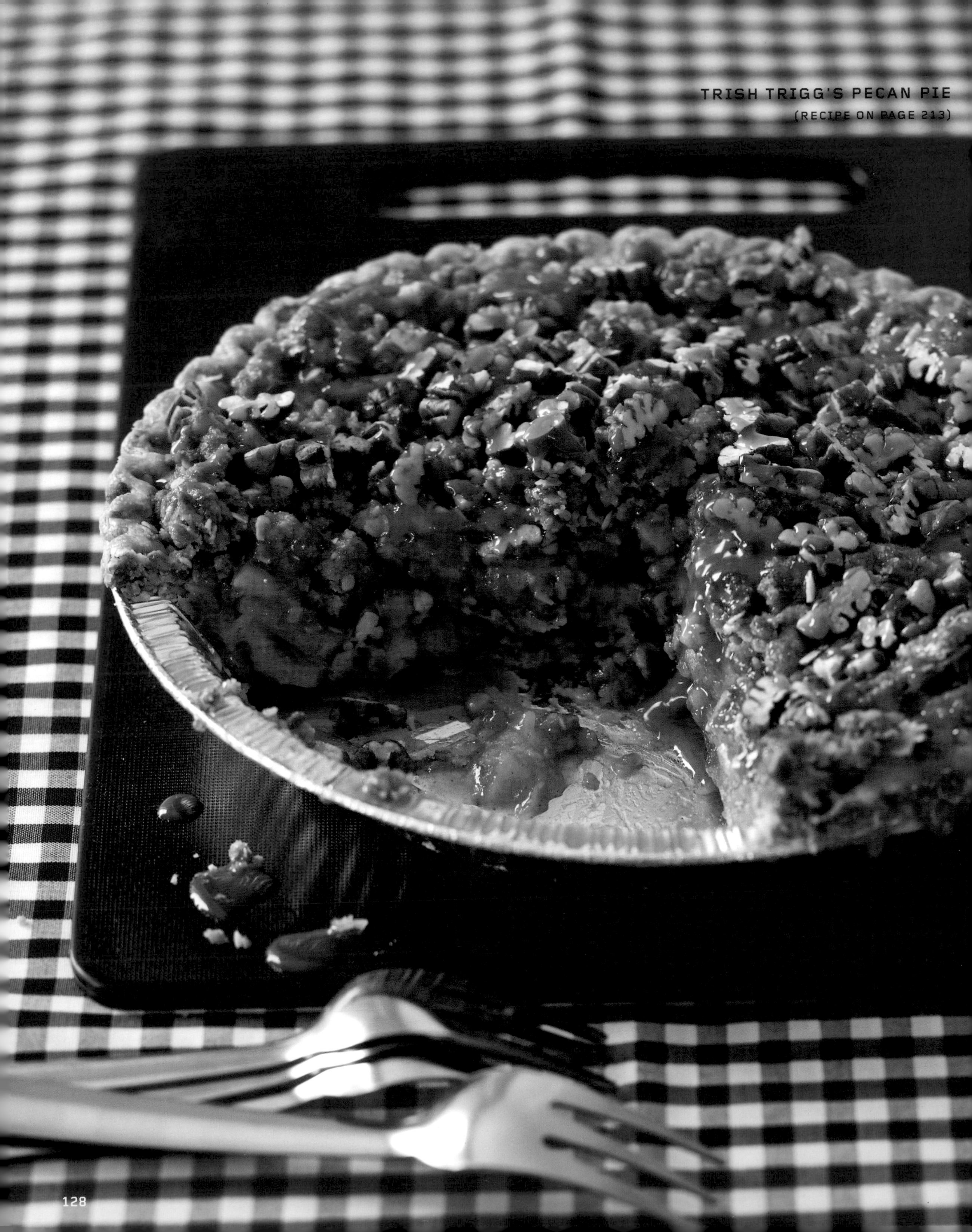

TRISH TRIGG'S PECAN PIE

(RECIPE ON PAGE 213)

Bratwurst with Beer, Butter, and Onions

I've cooked and eaten a lot of brats in Wisconsin and I've found that this is the best way to cook them.

½ cup (4 ounces) butter

12 links fresh bratwurst

1 large onion, thinly sliced

One 12-ounce can of beer (whatever you're drinking will be fine), or more as needed

12 brat buns

Mustard, for serving (optional)

Prepare the grill for cooking over direct medium heat. Place a deep 9-x-13-inch disposable aluminum pan on one side of the grill and add the stick of butter. Put the brats on the other side of the grill, directly on the grate. When the butter melts, add the sliced onion to the pan. Toss the onion occasionally. Flip the brats as needed. When the onions get soft, add the can of beer. As the brats get nicely browned, add them to the pan. Don't worry about them being done all the way because they are going to continue to cook in the pan. You can add more beer if it's needed, but we want to reduce it down by the end, so don't add too much.

When everything is in the pan, close the lid on the grill and cook for 15 minutes. Check the brats and continue cooking until everything in the pan is reduced to just soft onion and brats. This should take about another 15 minutes. Remove from the heat. Serve the brats on the rolls, topped with the onion and mustard, if desired.

MAKES 12 SANDWICHES

Washington Redskins

HOME STADIUM

FedEx Field
1600 Raljon Road
Landover, MD 20785

CAPACITY

91,665

OFFICIAL WEB SITE

www.redskins.com

FIRST GAME PLAYED

September 16, 1937

CHAMPIONSHIPS

NFL/NFC Champions 1937, 1942, 1972, 1982, 1983, 1987, 1991

Super Bowl Champions 1982, 1987, 1991

SIGNATURE FOOD OF THE AREA

The power lunch

GREAT BARBECUE

Old Glory BBQ

GREAT STEAKHOUSE

Bobby Van's Steakhouse

GREAT BREW

Dominion Ale

HALL OF FAMERS

George Allen, Coach, 1971–1977
Cliff Battles, RB, 1937
Sammy Baugh, QB, 1937–1952
Bill Dudley, RB, 1950–1951, 1953
Turk Edwards, OT, 1937–1940
Ray Flaherty, Coach, 1937–1942
Joe Gibbs, Coach, 1981–1992, 2004–present
Darrell Green, CB, 1983–2002
Ken Houston, CB, 1973–1980
Sam Huff, LB, 1964–1967, 1969
Deacon Jones, DE, 1974
Stan Jones, DT, 1966
Sonny Jurgensen, QB, 1964–1974
Paul Krause, S, 1964–1967
Curly Lambeau, Coach, 1952–1953
Vince Lombardi, Coach, 1969
Art Monk, WR, 1980–1993
George Preston Marshall, Owner, 1937–1969
Wayne Milner, WR, 1937–1941, 1945
Bobby Mitchell, WR, 1962–1968
John Riggins, RB, 1976–1979, 1981–1985
Charley Taylor, WR, 1964–1975, 1977

CHEERLEADERS

Redskins Cheerleaders

BEST SEASON

1983 & 1991 (14–2)

WASHINGTON, D.C., AND FOOD

Washington, D.C., is at the top of the list when it comes to the diversity of its people, and subsequently its food. With all the people who live there to do business with the American government, they have all the bases covered. You'll find just about any ethnic cuisine you could imagine and a couple you didn't even know about. But Washington is full of good old American expense accounts too, so you'll find plenty of big, fun, high-end dining all over town. Even some of the big-name chefs have found a home for their restaurants here. You can visit Michel Richard at Citronelle or go to Cindy Hutson's Ortanique for a great meal. There's a seaport nearby too, so expect wonderful fresh seafood in Washington, and with all the air traffic in and out, the best of everything from all over the world can be had there. Don't miss the big barbecue cook-off on Pennsylvania Avenue each June, where the best cooks from all over the country compete. Lots to see, do, and eat in Washington, D.C.

Here are my suggestions for what to cook for a Redskins Game-Day Party. Mix and match as you wish.

Grilled Vidalia Onion Salsa (page 38)

Strawberry-Jalapeño Chicken Wings (page 50)

Smoky Beef Stew (page 84)

Turkey Gravy Sandwiches with Homemade Cranberry Sauce (page 138)

Plank-Cooked Shrimp and Scallops (page 169)

Loaded Cornbread Casserole (page 208)

Zesty Roasted Garlic Mashed Potatoes (page 200)

Whiskey Girl's Caramel-Apple Pie (page 215)

Grilled Carne Asada Tacos

Here's my tailgate version of the classic Mexican steak served with a salsa/guacamole combo that I call Guacasalsa. The Chipotle Pinto Beans on page 199 are a perfect accompaniment.

CARNE ASADA MARINADE

2 limes, juiced

¼ cup olive oil

2 cloves garlic, minced

1 serrano chile, seeded and minced

2 tablespoons finely chopped fresh cilantro leaves

1 tablespoon ancho chile powder

1 tablespoon ground cumin

1 tablespoon salt

1 teaspoon brown sugar

1 teaspoon black pepper

2 pounds skirt steak

8 green onions

18 six-inch corn or flour tortillas, warmed

Guacasalsa (facing page)

Hot sauce, as needed

In a medium bowl, whisk together all the marinade ingredients. Cut the steak into pieces about 6 inches long. Pound each piece with the flat side of a mallet to tenderize it. Dredge the pieces through the marinade and place them in a zip-top bag. When all the pieces are in the bag, add the rest of the marinade to the bag. Squeeze out as much air as you can and seal the bag. Refrigerate for at least 4 hours and up to 24. Occasionally work the meat around a little in the bag.

Prepare a grill for cooking over direct high heat. Grill the green onions for a minute or two, turning often. Remove them and chop them coarsely. Grill the steak pieces hot and fast for 1 to 2 minutes per side. They must be served rare. Remove to a platter as they are done. When all the steak is on the platter, cover it loosely with foil and let it rest for 5 minutes. Slice it thinly across the grain. Serve with the tortillas, Guacasalsa, grilled green onions, and your favorite hot sauce on the side.

MAKES 18 TACOS

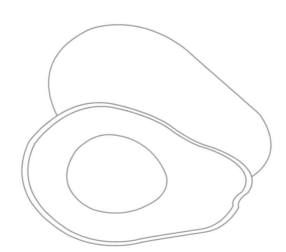

Guacasalsa

This is a perfect topping for the Carne Asada Tacos, but it's also great with chips.

2 Hass avocados, peeled, pitted, and diced

4 large Roma tomatoes, seeded and diced

1 small red onion, diced

1 lime, juiced

¼ cup chopped fresh cilantro leaves, more or less as you like

3 cloves garlic, crushed

1 serrano chile, minced (you may remove the seeds and veins if you want to remove the heat)

1 tablespoon salt

2 teaspoons black pepper

In a glass bowl, toss all the ingredients together. Cover and refrigerate for at least 4 hours, tossing occasionally to blend the flavors.

MAKES ABOUT 2 CUPS

Chipotle Chicken Tacos

This recipe calls for leftover smoked chicken, but I usually cook some chicken just so I can make these. If you don't want to cook the chicken, just pick up a rotisserie chicken at the grocery store.

2 tablespoons butter

2 cups chopped cooked chicken (leftover grilled or smoked chicken is best)

½ cup chicken broth

2 large canned chipotles in adobo sauce, finely chopped

8 six-inch flour or corn tortillas

Shredded cheese, diced tomatoes, chopped onion, and chopped shredded lettuce, for serving

In a skillet over medium heat, melt the butter. Add the chicken and cook for 3 to 4 minutes, breaking it up if needed. Add the broth and chipotles, stirring to blend well. Cover and cook for about 5 minutes, stirring occasionally. Remove the lid and add a little more broth if needed. Warm the tortillas briefly in the microwave or on the grill. Divide the chicken among the tortillas and serve with the cheese, tomatoes, onion, and lettuce, letting the guests dress their tacos as they like.

MAKES 8 TACOS

Catfish Tacos
with Citrus Salsa

A great way to serve catfish at the game. (Pictured on page 113.)

¼ cup all-purpose flour

1 tablespoon good-quality chili powder

1 teaspoon seasoned salt

1 teaspoon black pepper

1 pound catfish fillets, patted dry with a paper towel

2 tablespoons vegetable oil

2 tablespoons butter

8 six-inch flour or corn tortillas

Citrus Salsa (recipe follows)

In a small bowl, combine the flour, chili powder, salt, and pepper. Dust the fillets on both sides with the flour mixture.

Heat the oil and butter in a large skillet over medium-high heat. Put the fillets in the pan and cook for 4 to 5 minutes, then flip and cook another 4 to 5 minutes, or until the fish flakes when you poke it with a fork. Remove to drain on a paper towel. Transfer the fillets to a serving plate and break each into a few big pieces. Divide the fish evenly among the tortillas and top with the Citrus Salsa.

MAKES 8 TACOS

3 large Roma tomatoes, seeded and diced

½ cup finely chopped red onion

Supremes of 1 orange, chopped

Supremes of 1 large lime, chopped

3 green onions, white and green parts sliced

1 jalapeño, finely chopped (remove the seeds if you don't want it spicy)

2 tablespoons finely chopped fresh cilantro leaves

½ teaspoon salt

¼ teaspoon black pepper

Citrus Salsa

Using the supremes in this salsa leaves a little texture to the fruit while getting rid of the pith and skin. To make the supremes, just cut the top and bottom off of the fruit. Then stand it on one end and cut down the sides, removing the skin to reveal the fruit. All the skin and white pith should be removed. Now cut the segments out in between the membrane and pull out the tender wedge of flesh known as the supreme.

In a glass bowl, mix all the ingredients together. Cover and refrigerate for an hour. Mix again before serving.

MAKES ABOUT 2 CUPS

Grilled Tuna Sandwiches with Chipotle Mayo

I love grilled tuna, and the chipotle mayo makes it even better.

RUB

1 tablespoon sesame seeds

1 tablespoon good-quality chili powder

1 teaspoon salt

4 four-ounce tuna steaks

4 hamburger buns

CHIPOTLE MAYO

1 cup mayonnaise

3 tablespoons Tabasco Chipotle Sauce

4 leaves lettuce

4 slices onion

4 slices tomato

Prepare the grill for cooking over direct high heat.

In a small bowl, combine the rub ingredients and mix well. Sprinkle the rub evenly on both sides of the tuna steaks. Place the tuna on the grill for 1½ to 2 minutes, then flip and cook for the same amount on the other side. If your grill is hot enough, the tuna will be done perfectly. Most of the tuna should still be red when cut. Remove it to a plate to rest.

Quickly toast the buns on the grill. In a small bowl, mix together the mayonnaise with the Tabasco. Spread a thin layer on the top and bottom buns. Put a lettuce leaf on each bun bottom and top with a tuna steak, a slice of onion, a slice of tomato, and the top of the bun.

MAKES 4 SANDWICHES

Baltimore Ravens

HOME STADIUM

M&T Bank Stadium
1101 Russell Street
Baltimore, MD 21230

CAPACITY

70,008

OFFICIAL WEB SITE

www.baltimoreravens.com

FIRST GAME PLAYED

September 1, 1996

CHAMPIONSHIPS

AFC Champions 2000

Super Bowl Champions 2000

SIGNATURE FOOD OF THE AREA

Blue crabs/crab cakes

GREAT BARBECUE

Chaps Pit Beef

GREAT STEAKHOUSE

The Prime Rib

GREAT BREW

Clipper City Gold Ale

HALL OF FAMERS

None

CHEERLEADERS

Baltimore Ravens Cheerleaders

BEST SEASON

2006 (13–3)

BALTIMORE AND FOOD

The Ravens are a new team, but there's no shortage of football history in Baltimore and no shortage of food either. The steamed crabs and crab cakes are wonderful and available everywhere. These folks just love those crabs. You'll have no problem getting a local to teach you how to "pick" the sweet crabmeat, but they do it so much better than I can, so I just opt for the crab cakes that are made using meat that someone else has extracted. There's another great food tradition in Baltimore, and this one involves large chunks of meat cooked over fire. When I get to Baltimore, my first food stop is usually Chaps for a pit-beef sandwich. This is Baltimore's version of barbecue and it's great stuff. A pit-beef sandwich is a charred piece of roast beef that is sliced thinly and served on a roll. If you can't cook on game day, go to Chaps.

Here are my suggestions for what to cook for a Ravens Game-Day Party. Mix and match as you wish.

Crabby Crab Cakes (page 62)

Wing Ding Dry Rub Wings (page 47)

The Best Crab Soup Ever (page 79)

Steak Sandwiches on Garlic Bread with Grilled Onions (page 110)

Fancy Crab and Swiss Quiche (page 148)

Grapes and Yogurt Salad (page 193)

Baked Macaroni and Cheese (page 209)

Loaded Brownies (page 221)

Turkey Gravy Sandwiches with Homemade Cranberry Sauce

This is a perfect way to serve turkey and cranberry sauce to a crowd on game day. The Zesty Roasted Garlic Mashed Potatoes on page 200 are a perfect side dish.

One 14-pound turkey, fully defrosted

6 tablespoons olive oil, divided

1 teaspoon salt, plus more for the turkey

1 teaspoon black pepper, plus more for the turkey

2 carrots, peeled and cut in half

2 stalks celery, chopped

1 medium onion, chopped

One 14-ounce can chicken broth

One 14-ounce can vegetable broth

1 cup water

1 teaspoon rubbed (dried) sage

1 teaspoon dried thyme

1 bay leaf

½ cup all-purpose flour mixed with ½ cup water

15 to 20 hamburger or kaiser buns

Homemade Cranberry Sauce (facing page)

Preheat the oven to 325°F. Cut the tips and middle joints of the wings and the tail off of the turkey and set them aside. Remove the giblets and neck from the turkey and set them aside. Rub 3 tablespoons of the oil all over the turkey, then salt and pepper it inside and out. Put the turkey on a rack in a roaster and put it in the oven. Cook for about 3 hours, or to an internal temp of 160°F in the breast and 180°F in the thigh.

Meanwhile, make the gravy. In a Dutch oven, heat the remaining 3 tablespoons of the oil over medium heat. Add the wing tips, neck, tail, and giblets and brown well. Remove them to a plate. Add the carrots, celery, and onion to the pan and cook until the onion is soft, about 5 minutes, stirring often. Add the wing tips, neck, tail, and giblets back to the pot. Add both broths, the water, 1 teaspoon salt, 1 teaspoon pepper, the sage, thyme, and bay leaf. Bring to a simmer, stirring occasionally. Cover and simmer gently for 2 hours.

With a big slotted spoon, remove the carrots, wing tips, neck, tail, giblets, and bay leaf from the pot. Turn the heat off until the turkey is ready. Meanwhile, as the wings, neck, tail, and giblets cool, remove all the meat from them, chop the giblets, and return the meat and chopped giblets to the pot. Eat the carrots.

When the turkey is done, remove it to a platter and add the pan drippings to the gravy. Let the turkey cool for 30 minutes. While the turkey is resting, heat the stock back up. After it returns to a simmer, add the flour-water mixture and stir well. Continue cooking until it has thickened to a nice gravy consistency. You may need to add a little water or you may need to cook it down for a while. After the turkey has rested, pull it apart, removing all the meat from the bones. Chop and slice the meat into a texture that will be good for sandwiches. Transfer the turkey to a big pan. If you're doing this ahead for the game, let the gravy cool before adding it to the turkey, but if you're eating it right away, add the gravy to the pan now. When the gravy is added, toss the meat to coat it well. Cover with foil.

At this time you can refrigerate the turkey or heat it to serve. If heating it, preheat the oven to 350°F. Cook the turkey for 30 minutes and serve. If refrigerating, you'll need to reheat at 350°F for about an hour, or until warm and bubbling. After 30 minutes the turkey should be stirred. Serve on buns with Homemade Cranberry Sauce.

MAKES 15 TO 20 SANDWICHES

Homemade Cranberry Sauce

The apricots make this sauce very special. Don't save it only for turkey.

1 cup orange juice

½ cup granulated sugar

½ cup packed brown sugar

One 12-ounce package fresh cranberries

6 dried apricots, finely chopped

Zest of ½ lemon

In a medium saucepan over medium heat, mix together the orange juice and sugars, stirring often. When the sugars melt, add the cranberries, apricots, and lemon zest. Bring to a boil, stirring often, and then reduce the heat to a simmer. Cook for about 15 minutes, stirring often, until the cranberries begin to break up and become part of the sauce. Transfer to a bowl and serve.

MAKES ABOUT 3 CUPS

Judy's Double-Stuffed Cheeseburgers

My friend Judy made these burgers for me. They have the toppings on the inside. They're big, but you can cut them in half to serve.

1 medium, ripe tomato

2 pounds ground chuck

8 slices mozzarella cheese

Salt, as needed

Red pepper flakes, as needed

Your favorite barbecue rub, as needed

4 onion rolls, split

Slice the tomato thinly. Divide the ground beef into 8 equal portions. Flatten each portion into a thin patty bigger than the tomato slices. Trim the mozzarella slices into the same shape and size as the tomatoes. On top of 4 of the patties, lay a slice of cheese and a slice of tomato. Sprinkle the tomato with salt and red pepper flakes. Top with another slice of cheese and another ground beef patty. Now crimp the edges and shape the burgers, making sure the edges are sealed. Sprinkle the burgers on both sides with the rub. If you're taking these to the game, put them in a single layer, covered, in the refrigerator.

When it's time to cook them, prepare the grill for cooking over direct medium heat. Grill the burgers until browned on both sides and the meat reaches an internal temp of 155°F. This should take 5 to 7 minutes per side, depending on your grill. Transfer to the onion buns.

MAKES 4 BIG CHEESEBURGERS

Ray's Tropical Pork Chop Sandwiches

You'll be dreaming you're in the islands when you try these. The Key lime juice is readily available in a bottle and the guava paste will be in the aisle with Spanish ingredients. If you can't find them near you, both items will be easy to find online.

MARINADE

½ cup pineapple juice

½ cup canned coconut milk

¼ cup finely chopped red onion

3 tablespoons coconut rum

1 tablespoon Key lime juice

1 clove garlic, crushed

1 teaspoon guava paste

1 teaspoon salt

1 teaspoon black pepper

1 teaspoon paprika

¼ teaspoon vanilla extract

Pinch nutmeg

8 boneless pork loin chops, about ¾ inch thick

8 sandwich rolls

8 slices pineapple

8 slices red bell pepper

To make the marinade: Whisk together all the marinade ingredients. Put the pork chops in a zip-top bag or a glass bowl and pour the marinade over them. Toss to coat well. Marinate in the refrigerator for 24 hours, tossing occasionally to coat evenly.

Prepare the grill for cooking over direct medium-high heat. Grill the chops, turning once or twice, until done to an internal temperature of 150°F. Any higher and they will quickly become tough and dry. Place each pork chop on a bun. Quickly grill the pineapple slices for 1 minute on each side and put them on top of the pork chops. Top each with a slice of red pepper and serve.

MAKES 8 SANDWICHES

Buffalo Chicken Breast Sandwiches

I think the folks in Buffalo are gonna love these. (Pictured on page 117.)

6 boneless chicken breast halves

Your favorite barbecue rub

1 cup Frank's Red Hot Sauce

¼ cup (2 ounces) butter, melted

6 sandwich rolls

1½ cups crumbled blue cheese

1 cup finely chopped celery

Prepare the grill for cooking over direct medium-high heat. Season the chicken breasts lightly with the rub. Grill for about 5 minutes per side, or to an internal temperature of 160°F. Remove the chicken to a plate.

In a medium bowl, mix together the hot sauce and melted butter. Dip each chicken breast in the hot sauce mixture and transfer it to a rack to drain for just a minute. Transfer the chicken to the rolls and top each with an equal portion of the cheese and celery.

MAKES 6 SANDWICHES

BCT Sandwiches

I don't really like lettuce, so I substituted chicken for it in these sandwiches. I think they're much better than the original.

MARINADE

2 tablespoons vegetable oil

2 tablespoons soy sauce

2 tablespoons Worcestershire sauce

2 tablespoons ketchup

1 teaspoon black pepper

6 boneless skinless chicken thighs

12 slices toast

12 slices bacon, cooked and cut in half

12 thin slices tomato

Mayo, as needed

To make the marinade: In a medium bowl, whisk together all the ingredients. Put the thighs in a zip-top bag or a glass container and pour the marinade over them. Toss well to coat. Marinate in the refrigerator for at least 2 hours, and preferably overnight.

Prepare the grill for cooking over direct medium heat. Remove the thighs from the marinade and grill them for 12 to 15 minutes, turning often, or until they reach an internal temperature of 180°F. Put each thigh on a piece of toast. Top each sandwich with 4 pieces of bacon and 2 slices of tomato. Spread a thin layer of mayo on the top slice of toast and put it on. Cut in half to serve.

MAKES 6 SANDWICHES

Eggless Egg Salad Sandwiches

Here's a good one for the vegetarians in the crowd.

One 1-pound block firm tofu

½ cup plain yogurt

⅓ cup minced celery

2 tablespoons sweet pickle cubes

2 tablespoons minced green onion

1 teaspoon yellow mustard

¼ teaspoon salt

¼ teaspoon pepper

12 slices whole wheat bread

Drain the tofu and pat it dry. In a medium bowl, with a cheese grater, grate the tofu. Gently mix in the remaining ingredients, except for the bread. Refrigerate for 1 hour. When ready to serve, divide the mixture evenly and spread it onto 6 slices of the bread. Top with the remaining bread and cut in half to serve.

MAKES 6 SANDWICHES

Homemade Meat Loaf Sandwiches

Just like grandma used to make.

1 cup cubed bread

½ cup milk

2 pounds lean ground beef

1 onion, minced

½ cup (2 ounces) grated mozzarella cheese

2 large eggs, lightly beaten

2 tablespoons chopped fresh parsley

2 cloves garlic, crushed

2 teaspoons salt

1 teaspoon dried oregano

1 teaspoon dried basil

½ teaspoon black pepper

⅔ cup marinara sauce

12 hamburger buns

Ketchup, as needed

Preheat the oven to 350°F. Combine the bread cubes and milk in a small bowl. Set them aside to soak.

In a large bowl, mix together the meat, onion, cheese, eggs, parsley, garlic, salt, oregano, basil, and pepper. Add the soaked bread cubes and mix thoroughly. Place the meat mixture on a double thickness of 12-x-18-inch sheets of foil. Shape the meat into a loaf. Pour the marinara sauce over the meat. Pull the foil up around the loaf and fold, pressing the foil together to form a tightly sealed pouch. Place it on a baking sheet and bake for 1½ hours, or until it reaches an internal temperature of 160°F. Remove the loaf from the oven, open the foil to release steam, and let it rest for 30 minutes. Refrigerate overnight.

Slice and serve the meat loaf on hamburger buns with ketchup.

MAKES 12 SANDWICHES

Buffalo Bills

HOME STADIUM

1 Bills Drive
Orchard Park, NY 14127

CAPACITY

73,967

OFFICIAL WEB SITE

www.buffalobills.com

FIRST GAME PLAYED

September 11, 1960

CHAMPIONSHIPS

AFL Champions 1964, 1965

AFC Champions 1990, 1991, 1992, 1993

SIGNATURE FOOD OF THE AREA

Buffalo chicken wings

GREAT BARBECUE

Lee's Barbeque

GREAT STEAKHOUSE

E. B. Green's Steakhouse

GREAT BREW

Flying Bison Buffalo Lager

HALL OF FAMERS

Joe DeLamielleure, G, 1973–1979, 1985
Jim Kelly, QB, 1986–1996
Marv Levy, Coach, 1986–1997
James Lofton, WR, 1989–1992
Billy Shaw, G, 1961–1969
O. J. Simpson, RB, 1969–1977
Thurman Thomas, RB, 1988–1999

CHEERLEADERS

Buffalo Jills

BEST SEASON

1964 (12–2)

BUFFALO AND FOOD

Buffalo is a workingman's town and there's plenty of diverse food, but for me it's all about the chicken wings. One of the finest game-day foods of all time was born here, and it should be in the Hall of Fame. In 1964 Teressa Bellissimo invented the Buffalo chicken wing to feed her son's friends at the Anchor Bar. Period. There isn't even a dispute over this one, so it makes it easy to go to the birthplace of this renowned football fan favorite, a pilgrimage all fans of NFL football and chicken wings should make. It's an unassuming place that serves the original Buffalo chicken wings. There are other wing joints all over Buffalo as well and many of them are very good. I like to try a few different ones because, while the original is a wonderful dish, it has created a global market for chicken wings that didn't exist before. Who knew the lowly chicken wing was so good with all kinds of big seasonings on it? I've included a few of my favorite recipes, but you really need to visit the Anchor Bar.

Here are my suggestions for what to cook for a Bills Game-Day Party. Mix and match as you wish.

Blue Cheese Veggie Dip (page 43) with celery sticks

Bloody Mary Chicken Wings (page 46)

Asian Orange Wings (page 51)

Warm-Up Beef Barley Soup (page 74)

Buffalo Chicken Breast Sandwiches (page 141)

Spicy Spare Ribs (page 155)

Chipotle Pinto Beans (page 199)

Creamy Coleslaw (page 195)

Sweet Blueberry-Apricot Crumble (page 227)

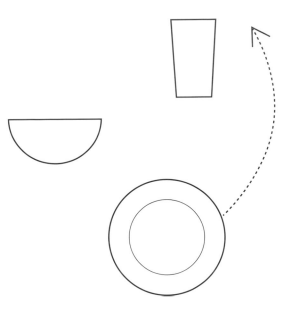

Exciting Entrées

I've never been happy to just serve something simple and common when I'm cooking for my friends. From the time I was a young man, I would spend all day cooking on Saturday for the Sunday morning game-day party in the parking lot. I'd cook ribs and scalloped potatoes and beans and cupcakes so everyone would enjoy the day. I remember the time I made my first homemade sausage and cooked it before a game at Soldier Field. Well, I put a little more garlic in than I should have, and while we sure enjoyed it, it was a good thing it was only the boys at the game that day! I'm sure I'm not the only one like this, though, because I've seen a guy cook shish kebabs on a grill next to the hatchback of his Porsche and I've seen guys cooking 24-ounce lobster tails while sipping on top-shelf gin in the parking lot next to their van.

While some days I'm perfectly happy with a cup of soup and a sandwich, other times it's fun to serve a nice entrée on game day. There's just no reason to simplify a meal just because we're eating outside. Hey, I'm a barbecue guy. And besides, I think rack of lamb tastes better when you eat it outside. Many of us have our game-day parties at home anyway, so a main course is a natural then. These are the things we all eat for Sunday dinner, so why not serve them during the big event of the week, the game? My Baked Ziti (page 183), for example, is an easy-to-serve, filling dish that can be heated at home and carried to a friend's house, the local bar, or the stadium with great success. I've also included a couple of great steak recipes to keep the carnivores happy, a fried turkey (it's not just for Thanksgiving anymore), one of my family's favorite recipes from my youth called Little Meats (page 161), and even an award-winning lobster recipe. Just like some football plays are basic and some are elaborate, so are the dishes we serve on game day.

Gringo Huevos Rancheros

This is my version of the classic. I like to use thickly sliced white bread—also known as Texas Toast—to corral the eggs.

6 slices Texas Toast—style bread

Cooking oil spray, for the griddle

¼ cup (2 ounces) unsalted butter, melted

6 large eggs

Salt, as needed

Black pepper, as needed

½ cup salsa

½ cup (2 ounces) grated Cheddar cheese

Preheat the broiler. Using a 2-inch cookie cutter, cut holes in the center of the bread slices, reserving the bread and the holes. Preheat a large griddle over medium heat. Lightly oil the griddle. Brush both sides of the bread slices and the holes with the melted butter. Place the bread and the holes on the griddle, keeping them separate. Crack an egg into the hole in each slice of bread. Cook for 3 minutes, or until the bread starts to toast and the egg starts to set. With a spatula, turn over the egg/bread combo and the holes. Sprinkle the tops lightly with salt and pepper. Cook for 3 minutes. Remove everything from the griddle to a baking sheet. If you couldn't do them all at once, repeat the process until all the eggs and toast are done. Top each egg with a toasty hole, salsa, and grated cheese. Put them under the broiler until the cheese melts, about 1 minute.

MAKES 6 SERVINGS

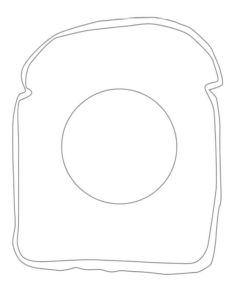

Fancy Crab and Swiss Quiche

This is a favorite of mine on Sunday morning. It's wonderful served at room temperature.

One unbaked 9-inch pie shell

1¼ cups (5 ounces) finely grated Swiss cheese

Two 6-ounce cans fancy lump crabmeat, drained

1 jalapeño, seeded and finely chopped

1 tablespoon all-purpose flour

3 green onions, thinly sliced

Pinch salt

½ teaspoon black pepper

3 large eggs

1 cup half-and-half

Preheat the oven to 350°F. Bake the pie shell for 10 minutes. Remove it from the oven to cool. Leave the oven on. When the shell is cooled, sprinkle half of the cheese in it. Flake the crab evenly over the cheese. Sprinkle the jalapeño over the crab. Sprinkle the flour over the jalapeño. Spread the remaining cheese evenly over the top. Sprinkle two-thirds of the green onions evenly over the cheese. Sprinkle the salt and pepper over the top. Beat together the eggs and half-and-half. Pour evenly over the top. Bake for 30 minutes, or until the quiche is set in the middle. Let it cool for 45 minutes. Top with the remaining green onions to serve. This is best served at room temperature.

MAKES 8 SERVINGS

Krystal Quiche

Krystals are little square burgers that we love in the South. Up north, they have White Castles that are equally good and can slide right in as a substitute in this recipe. And if you can't get either, look for the frozen White Castles at the grocery store.

Cooking oil spray, for the pan

12 Cheese Krystal Burgers, served with onions only

12 large eggs

½ cup milk

¼ teaspoon salt

½ teaspoon black pepper

Preheat the oven to 350°F. Spray a 9-x-13-inch baking pan with vegetable oil. Break the Krystals into small pieces (about 10 pieces per burger) and put them directly into the baking pan. In a large bowl, beat the eggs well with a whisk. Add the milk, salt, and pepper and mix well. Pour the egg mixture evenly over the Krystals. With the whisk, push the buns down so they all get soaked. Bake for 30 minutes, or until the eggs are all set. Let cool 5 minutes before serving.

MAKES 8 SERVINGS

Apricot-Stuffed Pork Roast

I love the taste of dried fruit with pork. This one can be done on the grill or in the oven.

One 3- to 4-pound boneless pork loin roast, cut to unroll in a jelly-roll fashion

2 tablespoons vegetable oil

¼ cup finely chopped onion

¼ cup finely chopped red bell pepper

¾ cup finely chopped dried apricots

2 tablespoons butter

½ teaspoon salt

½ teaspoon finely ground black pepper

1 teaspoon freshly grated lemon zest

1 tablespoon freshly squeezed lemon juice

3 tablespoons dried bread crumbs

Your favorite barbecue rub, as needed

Butcher string or any cotton string

Cutting the pork roast is best done by a butcher, but if you've got a sharp knife and are a little adventurous, you can do it. Just start on the bottom so you can hide the seam later. Take your time, cut all the way across the roast a little at a time, and unroll the roast as you go, making it as thin as you can.

In a large skillet over medium heat, warm the oil. Add the onion and bell pepper and cook for a minute or two, stirring occasionally, and then add the apricots and continue cooking until the onions are soft. Add the butter, salt, and pepper. Cook just until the butter is melted, stirring constantly. Remove from the heat and add the lemon zest and lemon juice. Mix well. Add as much of the bread crumbs as you need (discarding the rest) to soak up all the juices. Stir well. Transfer to a bowl and cool at room temperature for at least 30 minutes.

Preheat the oven to 350°F or prepare the grill for cooking over indirect medium heat, using apple wood for flavor. Unroll the prepared pork roast. Sprinkle the inside liberally with the rub. Spread the stuffing evenly over most of the flat roast, just leaving a 1-inch border all around without stuffing. Roll the roast back up, trying to shape it to a uniform thickness. Cut individual lengths of string and tie them around the roast every couple of inches. Do the ends first to hold the stuffing in. Try to keep the knots in a line for a nice presentation. Trim the loose ends of the string as close as you can with scissors. Season the outside of the roast liberally with the rub. Put the roast on a rack in a pan for the oven or directly on the grill.

Cook until the pork reaches an internal temperature of 145°F. This should take 1½ to 2 hours. Tent with foil and let it rest for 10 minutes. Slice it carefully, cutting and discarding the string as you go, to keep the slices together for a nice presentation.

MAKES 8 SERVINGS

Maple Pork
on a Maple Plank

Maple syrup and the smokiness from the maple plank make this dish a winner. Cedar planks started the plank cooking craze and those will work if you can't find maple, but any grill store should have a variety of wood types available.

Two 1-pound pork tenderloins

½ cup (4 ounces) butter, melted

½ cup plus 2 tablespoons maple syrup, divided

1 teaspoon dry mustard

½ teaspoon cayenne

Your favorite barbecue rub, as needed

1 maple cooking plank, soaked in water for 1 hour

Trim all the fat and silver skin from the tenderloins. Mix together the butter, ½ cup of the maple syrup, the dry mustard, and cayenne. With a kitchen injector, inject the mixture evenly throughout both tenderloins. Season the tenderloins liberally with the rub. Put the tenderloins in a zip-top bag and refrigerate for at least 1 hour and up to 12 hours.

Prepare the grill for cooking over direct medium-high heat. Put the tenderloins on the plank so they aren't touching each other. Put the plank on the grill and cover the grill. Cook for about 1 hour, or until the tenderloins reach an internal temperature of 150°F. Remove the whole plank to a baking sheet. Drizzle the pork with the remaining 2 tablespoons of maple syrup. Tent it loosely with aluminum foil. Let the pork rest for 5 minutes. Slice and serve right on the plank.

MAKES 6 SERVINGS

Cincinnati Bengals

HOME STADIUM

Paul Brown Stadium
One Paul Brown Stadium
Cincinnati, OH 45204

CAPACITY

65,535

OFFICIAL WEB SITE

www.bengals.com

FIRST GAME PLAYED

September 6, 1968

CHAMPIONSHIPS

AFC Champions 1981, 1988

SIGNATURE FOOD OF THE AREA

Cincinnati chili

GREAT BARBECUE

City BBQ

GREAT STEAKHOUSE

Jeff Ruby's Steakhouse

GREAT BREW

Little Kings

HALL OF FAMERS

Paul Brown, Coach, 1968–1975
Charlie Joiner, WR, 1972–1975
Anthony Munoz, OT, 1980–1992

CHEERLEADERS

Ben-Gals

BEST SEASON

1981 & 1988 (12–4)

CINCINNATI AND FOOD

Cincinnati is a big city, a river city, an old city, a vibrant city, and a city right across the river from Kentucky. That's a lot of hats to wear, but Cincinnati wears them well. This city also has a nickname. It's known as "Porkopolis" because it was the early pork center of the United States. Those days are gone, but you can still get a good pork chop there. But the real food story there is the chili. It's not like the chili anywhere else. It's brown and thin and the meat is finely ground and it seems more like a sauce than a bowl of red, but that's OK with me. It's typically served on thin spaghetti noodles with cheese for "three-way," plus beans and onions for "five-way." It's an acquired taste, but it's been acquired by a lot of folks. I can buy it in the freezer section here in Florida, and I always stop for a plate when changing planes at the Cincinnati airport. It's different, but it's good!

Here are my suggestions for what to cook for a Bengals Game-Day Party. Mix and match as you wish.

Stuffed Jalapeños Wrapped in Bacon (page 63)

Barbecued Chicken Nachos (page 52)

Dr. BBQ's Grandma's Chicken Dumpling Soup (page 70)

Bratwurst with Beer, Butter, and Onions (page 129)

Apricot-Stuffed Pork Roast (page 150)

Barbecue Pit Beans (page 200)

Warm German Potato Salad (page 195)

White-Bottom Pumpkin Pie (page 213)

Peachy Baby Back Ribs

Everybody loves sweet, sticky barbecued ribs. These are a little different and served without barbecue sauce, but feel free to add some if you like. (Pictured on page 121.)

½ cup of your favorite barbecue rub

¼ cup turbinado sugar (Sugar in the Raw)

3 full slabs (about 2 pounds each) baby back ribs, back membrane removed

1½ cups peach preserves

6 tablespoons packed brown sugar

¾ cup apple juice

Mix the rub and sugar together and sprinkle it on the ribs. Use about two-thirds on the meaty side and one-third on the boney side.

Prepare the grill for cooking over indirect low (300°F) heat, using peach wood or a combination of cherry and hickory for flavor.

Cook the ribs until they are nicely caramelized and looking great. This should take about 2 hours. Remove the ribs to a platter or sheet pan. Lay out 3 double-thick layers of heavy-duty aluminum foil, each big enough to wrap a whole slab. Transfer each slab of ribs to a piece of foil. Top each slab with ½ cup of the preserves. Sprinkle 2 tablespoons of brown sugar over each slab. As you fold each foil into a packet, pour ¼ cup of the juice in under the ribs. Seal the packets snugly, being careful not to puncture the foil with the rib bones. Return them to the grill for 45 minutes.

At this point, you could let the ribs cool down to finish later. This is a great way to take the ribs to a game-day party at a friend's house or at the game. To reheat them, put the cooked ribs on a direct medium-hot grill. Cook and flip them for just a few minutes, until they are warm and caramelized. Cut each slab into 3 pieces and serve.

MAKES 9 SERVINGS

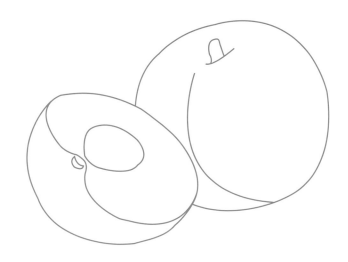

Spicy Spare Ribs

These are really just great barbecued ribs. You can skip the hot sauce
if you don't want them spicy.

Two 4-pound slabs spare ribs

Your favorite barbecue rub, as needed

½ cup apple juice, divided

2 cups of your favorite barbecue sauce

⅓ cup hot sauce or to your taste

Prepare the smoker or grill for cooking over indirect low (275°F) heat,
using 2 parts cherry wood and 1 part hickory wood for flavor.

Peel the membrane off the back of the ribs. Season the ribs liberally
with the rub. Place the ribs in the cooker, meaty-side up. Cook for about
3 hours, or until the ribs have a nice brown color and are beginning to get
soft. Remove the ribs from the cooker. Lay out a big double-thick layer of
heavy-duty aluminum foil for each slab. Lay the ribs on the foil meaty-side
up. As you begin to close up the foil into a package around the ribs, add
¼ cup of the apple juice to each packet. Now wrap the ribs up tightly, being
careful not to puncture the foil with the rib bones. Put the ribs back in the
cooker for another 1½ hours, or until they reach your desired degree of
tenderness.

Take the ribs out of the foil, and put them back on the cooker. Mix the
barbecue sauce with the hot sauce. Brush both sides of the ribs with some
of the barbecue sauce, and cook for another 20 minutes. Remove the ribs
to a platter and let them rest for 5 minutes. Lay each slab on a cutting
board, meaty-side down, and cut through the slab to separate every rib.
Transfer them to a platter and serve with the remaining sauce on the side.

MAKES 6 SERVINGS

Cleveland Browns

HOME STADIUM

Cleveland Browns Stadium
100 Alfred Lerner Way
Cleveland, OH 44114

CAPACITY

Over 73,200

OFFICIAL WEB SITE

www.clevelandbrowns.com

FIRST GAME PLAYED

September 16, 1950

CHAMPIONSHIPS

NFL Champions 1950, 1954, 1955, 1964

SIGNATURE FOOD OF THE AREA

Barbecue ribs

GREAT BARBECUE

Hot Sauce Williams

GREAT STEAKHOUSE

Cabin Club Steak House

GREAT BREW

Dortmunder Gold Lager

HALL OF FAMERS

Doug Atkins, DE, 1953–1954
Jim Brown, FB, 1957–1965
Paul Brown, Coach, 1946–1962
Willie Davis, DE, 1958–1959
Len Dawson, QB, 1960–1961
Joe DeLamielleure, G, 1980–1984
Len Ford, DE, 1950–1957
Frank Gatski, C, 1946–1956
Otto Graham, QB, 1946–1955
Lou Groza, T/PK, 1946–1959, 1961–1967
Gene Hickerson, G, 1958–1973
Henry Jordan, DT, 1957–1958
Leroy Kelly, RB, 1964–1973
Dante Lavelli, E, 1946–1956
Mike McCormick, T, 1954–1962
Tommy McDonald, WR, 1968
Bobby Mitchell, WR, 1958–1961
Marion Motley, FB, 1946–1953
Ozzie Newsome, TE, 1978–1990
Paul Warfield, WR, 1964–1969, 1976–1977
Bill Willis, G, 1946–1953

CHEERLEADERS

None

BEST SEASON

1951 & 1953 (11–1)

CLEVELAND AND FOOD

Like so many of the well-established cities of the North, Cleveland is a melting pot. A quick look at the lineup for the Taste of Cleveland festival, over Labor Day weekend, shows everything that Greek, Indian, German, Polish, Mexican, Italian, and even Cajun food will offer. That's quite a diverse menu. There is another food phenomenon in Cleveland and it's known as a ribfest. These have become common now all around the country, but it all started in Cleveland in the 1980s when a group of rib cooks gathered to see who made the best ribs and to sell a few while they were at it. The customers thought this was a great idea and the concept has grown and prospered all over the country ever since, but to this day Cleveland remains the home to some of the biggest and best ribfests. If you attend one of these great events around the country, be sure to face Cleveland as you bite your first rib because that's where it all began.

Here are my suggestions for what to cook for a Browns Game-Day Party. Mix and match as you wish.

Sweet Sticky Barbecue Salsa (page 38)

Barbecued Chicken Nachos (page 52)

Dr. BBQ's Championship Chili (page 98)

Barbecued Bologna Sandwiches (page 110)

Peachy Baby Back Ribs (page 154)

Creamy Coleslaw (page 195)

Barbecue Pit Beans (page 200)

Barbara Lowe's Cook-Off Orange Bars (page 220)

Asian Sauced Ribs

I like these for a different taste in ribs, but you can substitute your favorite barbecue sauce and they'll be traditional barbecued ribs.

Three 2½-pound slabs baby back or St. Louis–style ribs, membranes removed

Your favorite barbecue rub, as needed

ASIAN RIB SAUCE

½ cup hoisin sauce

¼ cup soy sauce

¼ cup honey

¼ cup rice vinegar

¼ teaspoon white pepper

¾ cup apple juice

Season the ribs liberally with the barbecue rub. Cover and refrigerate for up to 4 hours.

To make the sauce: In a small bowl, whisk together the ingredients. Cover and set aside. Prepare the grill for cooking over indirect low (275°F) heat.

Cook the ribs until they are nicely caramelized and looking great. This should take about 2 hours. Remove the ribs to a platter or sheet pan. Lay out 3 double-thick layers of heavy-duty aluminum foil, each big enough to wrap a whole slab. Transfer each slab of ribs to a piece of foil. As you fold each foil into a packet, pour ¼ cup of the juice in under the ribs. Seal the packets snugly, being careful not to puncture the foil with the rib bones. Return them to the grill for 1 hour, or until tender to the touch.

At this point, you could let the ribs cool down to finish later. This is a great way to take the ribs to a game-day party at a friend's house or at the game. To reheat them, put the cooked ribs on a direct medium-hot grill. Cook and flip them for just a few minutes, until they are warm and caramelized. Brush with the Asian Rib Sauce and cook for just a few minutes or they will burn. Cut each slab into 3 pieces and serve.

MAKES 9 SERVINGS

Barbecue Championship Rack of Lamb

I made this dish up on the spot for the Barbecue Championship Series TV show on the Versus network. It scored very well that day and will score very well at any game-day party.

¼ cup of your favorite barbecue rub

2 tablespoons good-quality chili powder

Three 1½-pound racks of lamb, trimmed

RASPBERRY-BALSAMIC REDUCTION

1 quart balsamic vinegar

½ cup raspberry preserves

¼ cup (2 ounces) butter

Salt, as needed

Black pepper, as needed

Wood chips (hickory preferred), soaked in water for 1 hour

In a small bowl, mix together the rub and the chili powder. Season the lamb liberally with the rub-chili blend. Return the lamb to the refrigerator.

In a small saucepan, cook the vinegar over low heat, reducing it to 1 cup. This will take about 30 minutes. Add the preserves, butter, and salt and pepper to taste, and mix well until blended. Set aside.

Prepare the grill for cooking over direct high heat. Drain the wood chips and put them on top of the hot coals, or in the appropriate place for your grill. Grill the lamb on all sides until well browned and it reaches an internal temperature of 130°F for medium-rare. Brush the racks with the reduction for the last few minutes to glaze. Slice the lamb between each bone and drizzle with more reduction to serve.

MAKES 6 SERVINGS

Garlic-Infused
Leg of Lamb

A Sunday dinner favorite with my family. Cooking the lamb on the bone gives it great flavor.

ROASTED GARLIC

1 large head garlic

Olive oil, as needed

Pinch of salt

One 5- to 6-pound bone-in leg of lamb

3 tablespoons olive oil, divided

Freshly grated zest of 1 lemon

1 tablespoon dried oregano

½ teaspoon salt, plus more as needed

½ teaspoon ground black pepper, plus more as needed

Preheat the oven to 350°F.

Cut the top off the head of garlic, exposing the tops of the cloves. Put the garlic in a small baking pan. Drizzle it with oil and sprinkle with salt. Bake for 25 minutes, or until soft. Remove it from the oven to cool.

With a sharp knife, stab the lamb every few inches, making an X in each of about 12 spots. Squeeze the garlic out of its skin onto a cutting board. Chop it finely. In a small bowl, combine the garlic, 2 tablespoons of the olive oil, the lemon zest, oregano, ½ teaspoon salt, and ½ teaspoon pepper into a paste. With your fingers, stuff some of the paste deep into each of the slits in the lamb. Rub the last tablespoon of oil and any leftover paste all over the lamb. Season the outside with salt and pepper. Put the lamb on a rack in a roasting pan. Cook the lamb for about 2 hours, or until the lamb reaches an internal temperature of 150°F for medium. Remove it from the oven, tent loosely with foil, and let it rest for 10 minutes. Slice and serve.

MAKES 10 SERVINGS

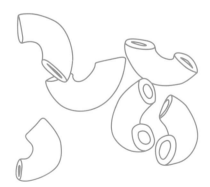

Little Meats

This is one of the recipes I got from my Grandma Julia. My sister Denise and I have been eating it all of our lives and still love it. I don't know where the name came from—it's really just macaroni and beef, but at my house it's always called Little Meats.

2 pounds ground chuck

1 small onion, finely chopped

1 cup water

One 8-ounce can tomato sauce

One 6-ounce can tomato paste

2 teaspoons seasoned salt

1 teaspoon black pepper

8 ounces elbow macaroni, cooked

In a Dutch oven over medium-high heat, sauté the ground beef and onion, crumbling the beef and stirring occasionally, until the meat is cooked through, 8 to 10 minutes. Do not drain the meat. Add the water, tomato sauce, tomato paste, salt, and pepper and stir well. Bring to a boil, reduce the heat to a simmer, cover, and cook for 20 minutes, stirring occasionally. Remove the cover and cook for another 10 minutes. To serve, spoon over the cooked macaroni.

MAKES 8 SERVINGS

Mini Meat Loaves

Everybody loves meat loaf and these mini versions make a great game-day entrée. These go very well with macaroni and cheese.

3 tablespoons vegetable oil

1 medium onion, chopped

1 large green bell pepper, chopped

2 cloves garlic, crushed

3 pounds lean ground beef

3 large eggs, lightly beaten

½ cup prepared chili sauce

2 tablespoons soy sauce

2 tablespoons Worcestershire sauce

2 teaspoons salt

2 teaspoons black pepper

1 cup oatmeal

8 slices bacon, cut in half

Barbecue sauce, as needed

Preheat the oven to 350°F or prepare the grill for cooking over indirect medium heat.

In a medium skillet over medium heat, warm the oil. Add the onion, bell pepper, and garlic and cook, stirring occasionally for 5 minutes, or until the onion begins to soften. Remove the pan from the heat and set aside. Crumble the beef into a large bowl. Add the eggs, chili sauce, soy sauce, Worcestershire, salt, and pepper. Using your hands, mix well. Add the oatmeal and mix well. Divide the mixture among 8 mini meat loaf pans. Top each loaf with 2 half slices of bacon. Place the loaves in the oven or on the grill, covered, and cook for 40 minutes, or until they reach an internal temperature of 155°F. Remove from the heat and let them rest for 5 minutes. Remove from the pans and serve with barbecue sauce on the side.

MAKES 8 SERVINGS

Down-Home Pot Roast with Potatoes and Carrots

Another Sunday dinner favorite that travels well.

¼ cup all-purpose flour

2 teaspoons salt, divided

1 teaspoon dried oregano

½ teaspoon paprika

1 teaspoon black pepper, divided

One 3-pound boneless chuck roast

¼ cup olive oil

1 cup sliced onions

1½ cups water

2 tablespoons Worcestershire sauce

4 medium white potatoes, peeled and cut into quarters

4 carrots, cut in 2-inch pieces

3 stalks celery, cut in 1-inch pieces

3 cloves garlic, minced

Preheat the oven to 325°F.

On a plate, combine the flour, 1 teaspoon of the salt, the oregano, paprika, and ½ teaspoon of the pepper. Dredge the roast in the flour mixture.

In a large skillet, heat the oil over medium-high heat. Add the onions and sauté for 3 minutes, then add the roast and brown it on all sides. Transfer the roast to a Dutch oven. Add the water and Worcestershire to the skillet with the onions. Bring it to a boil, scraping the bottom of the pan. Pour over the roast. Cover and bake for 1 hour. Add the potatoes, carrots, celery, garlic, remaining 1 teaspoon of salt, and remaining ½ teaspoon of pepper. Cover and bake for an additional 1 hour, or until everything is tender. Remove the roast from the oven and let it rest for 5 minutes. Remove the roast from the pot and slice. Transfer it to a serving platter, ladle the vegetables over, and serve.

MAKES 6 SERVINGS

Woodford-Marinated Rib-Eye Steaks

This is a bold, grown-up marinade for steaks and perfect for a tailgate party. I like to serve these with fresh tomato wedges, a twice-baked potato, and a glass of Woodford.

MARINADE

¼ cup of your favorite barbecue rub

¼ cup soy sauce

¼ cup Worcestershire sauce

¼ cup Woodford Reserve Premium Bourbon

1 teaspoon balsamic vinegar

1 teaspoon hot sauce

4 USDA Choice rib-eye steaks, about 12 ounces each

At least 4 hours before you plan to cook and preferably the night before, whisk all the marinade ingredients together in a bowl and set aside. Put the steaks in a zip-top bag (or two) and pour the marinade over them. Squeeze all of the air out of the bag and seal. Refrigerate until you're ready to cook, tossing occasionally to coat the meat evenly.

When you're ready to cook, prepare the grill for cooking over direct high heat. Take the steaks out of the marinade and put them directly on the grill. Discard the marinade. Cook for 3 to 4 minutes, or until nicely browned. Flip and cook for another 3 to 4 minutes, or until done to your liking.

MAKES 4 SERVINGS

Denver Broncos

HOME STADIUM

INVESCO Field at Mile High Stadium
1701 Bryant Street
Denver, CO 80204

CAPACITY

76,125

OFFICIAL WEB SITE

www.denverbroncos.com

FIRST GAME PLAYED

September 9, 1960

CHAMPIONSHIPS

AFC Champions 1977, 1986, 1987,
1989, 1997, 1998

Super Bowl Champions 1997, 1998

SIGNATURE FOOD OF THE AREA

Cowboy cuisine

GREAT BARBECUE

Dickey's

GREAT STEAKHOUSE

Gallagher's Steak House

GREAT BREW

Flying Dog Classic Pale Ale

HALL OF FAMERS

Willie Brown, CB, 1963–1966
Tony Dorsett, RB, 1988
John Elway, QB, 1983–1998
Gary Zimmerman, OT, 1993–1997

CHEERLEADERS

Denver Broncos Cheerleaders

BEST SEASON

1998 (14–2)

DENVER AND FOOD

When I think of Denver I think of the mountains. They're pretty hard to miss when you're right there. I also think of the Wild West and I see the food traditions that remain. There are plenty of Mexican foods and chicken-fried steaks, and you'll always see trout on the menu since there are so many streams there where they flourish. There's plenty of barbecue in Denver and plenty of steakhouses where they use that wonderful Colorado beef. I guess I'd call it American cuisine or maybe "cowboy cuisine." Whatever you call it, you'll find real stick-to-your-ribs food, and I like that. I'm sure there's some fancy cuisine in the city but that's not the face of Denver's cuisine. Just beware of the Rocky Mountain "oysters." They even serve them at the stadium. I'd suggest a lot of hot sauce, but really I think I'll just have a hot dog.

Here are my suggestions for what to cook for a Broncos Game-Day Party. Mix and match as you wish.

Nachos Ai Chihuahua (page 53)

Wing Ding Dry Rub Wings (page 47)

Game-Day Smoky Chili (page 99)

Steak Sandwiches on Garlic Bread with Grilled Onions (page 110)

Barbecued Chicken Legs with Raspberry-Chipotle Barbecue Sauce (page 176)

Chipotle Pinto Beans (page 199)

Zesty Roasted Garlic Mashed Potatoes (page 200)

Doenee's Nutella Bars (page 219)

Grilled Sirloin Steak
with Two-Mushroom Sauté

Sirloin is my favorite steak. This big one will feed quite a few hungry fans.
(Pictured on page 118.)

DR. BBQ'S SIRLOIN STEAK RUB

¼ cup salt

1 tablespoon ancho chile powder

1 tablespoon dry mustard

1 tablespoon paprika

2 teaspoons ground black pepper

1 teaspoon granulated garlic

1 teaspoon granulated onion

1 teaspoon ground coriander

One 2-pound sirloin steak

MUSHROOM SAUTÉ

½ cup olive oil

8 ounces white mushrooms, sliced

8 ounces baby portobello mushrooms,
sliced

1 small onion, finely chopped

2 Roma tomatoes, seeded and chopped

¼ cup red wine

1 jalapeño, finely chopped (seeds
optional)

1 tablespoon Dr. BBQ's Sirloin
Steak Rub

2 cloves garlic, crushed

Salt

To make the rub, in a small bowl, combine all the rub ingredients. It will make about 1 cup. You won't need the full amount of the rub for this recipe. Save the remaining rub in a sealed container at room temperature for later use.

Season the steak liberally on both sides with some of the rub. Set aside. Prepare the grill for cooking over direct medium-high heat.

In a large skillet over medium heat, warm the oil. Add the mushrooms, onion, tomatoes, wine, jalapeño, rub, and garlic and cook for 10 to 15 minutes, stirring often, until all the mushrooms are soft and the liquid is cooked off. Set aside. Grill the steak, turning it a few times, until it reaches an internal temperature of 145°F for medium-rare. Transfer it to a warm platter and let it rest for 5 minutes. Top with the mushroom mixture and serve.

MAKES 4 SERVINGS

Rockin' London Broil

My version of this classic has an Asian flair and it's rockin'.

MARINADE

¼ cup soy sauce (I like Kikkoman)

1 tablespoon Worcestershire sauce

1 tablespoon ketchup

2 cloves garlic, crushed

1½ teaspoons crushed fresh ginger

1½ teaspoons sherry

1½ teaspoons rice vinegar

½ teaspoon ground white pepper

One 2-pound top-round steak

To make the marinade, in a small bowl, whisk together all the ingredients. Put the steak in a zip-top bag and pour the marinade over it. Remove all the air and seal the bag. Refrigerate it for at least 4 hours and up to 24 hours.

Prepare the grill for cooking over direct high heat. Discard the marinade. Grill the steak to a doneness of no more than medium rare (130°F) and preferably rare (120°F). Any more and it will be tough. This should take 3 to 4 minutes per side, depending on your grill. Remove the steak to a cutting board and let it rest for 3 to 4 minutes, then slice it thinly and on an angle to go across the grain.

MAKES 8 SERVINGS

Garlic-Grilled Tri-Tip

Tri-tip is one of those things that is in every store in some areas of the country and can't be found in others. In California it is everywhere and in Florida I can't find one. It is part of the sirloin and it's really tasty so if you can find one give it a try.

1 head garlic, roasted (see page 160)

1 tri-tip roast, about 3 pounds

Your favorite barbecue rub, as needed

2 tablespoons (1 ounce) butter, melted

The morning you plan to cook, remove the garlic from the husk and chop it finely into a paste. Rub the garlic all over the tri-tip. Season the tri-tip liberally with the rub. Cover and refrigerate until it's time to cook.

Prepare the grill for cooking over indirect high heat, using oak wood for flavor. Place the tri-tip directly on the grate. Flip after 30 minutes and cook for 20 minutes more, or until it reaches an internal temp of 125°F. Remove to a platter. Brush it with the butter. Tent the meat loosely with foil and let it rest for 15 minutes. Slice it thinly across the grain and serve.

MAKES 4 SERVINGS

Shrimp Étouffée

Dr. BBQ's version of a New Orleans favorite. The word *étouffée* means "smothered" in French, as this big bold gravy smothers the shrimp.

½ cup (4 ounces) butter

¾ cup all-purpose flour

1½ cups chopped onion

¾ cup chopped celery

¾ cup chopped green bell pepper

½ cup grated carrot

2 cloves garlic, crushed

½ cup water

One 14-ounce can chicken broth

One 15-ounce can diced tomatoes

2 tablespoons Creole seasoning

½ teaspoon salt

½ teaspoon dried thyme

¼ teaspoon black pepper

¼ teaspoon cayenne

2 bay leaves

2 pounds large raw shrimp, peeled and deveined

½ cup chopped green onion

3 tablespoons chopped fresh parsley

Steamed, hot white rice, for serving

In a large skillet over medium-high heat, melt the butter. Gradually whisk in the flour. Continue to whisk the flour and butter mixture until it turns golden brown, 8 to 10 minutes. Reduce the heat to medium. With a large spoon, stir in the onion, celery, bell pepper, carrot, and garlic. Stir until the vegetables are heated through, about 3 minutes. Add the water and stir for 1 minute. Add the broth and tomatoes, and stir for 1 minute. Add the seasoning, salt, thyme, pepper, and cayenne. Bring the mixture to a simmer, and add the bay leaves. Bring the mixture to a boil, reduce the heat to a simmer, cover, and cook for 30 minutes, stirring occasionally. Add the shrimp and cook just until the shrimp turn pink, about 8 minutes. Stir in the green onion and parsley. Turn off the heat and let the étouffée rest for 5 minutes. Remove the bay leaves. Serve over steamed, hot rice.

MAKES 8 SERVINGS

Plank-Cooked Shrimp and Scallops

Plank cooking has become very popular. It's a fun way to serve the food and adds a nice flavor.

Two cedar cooking planks, soaked in water for 1 hour

1 lemon, thinly sliced

12 colossal raw shrimp, peeled and deveined

12 jumbo sea scallops

½ cup (4 ounces) butter, melted

1 teaspoon salt

1 teaspoon lemon pepper

1 teaspoon paprika

1 teaspoon granulated garlic

1 teaspoon dried thyme

6 green onions, sliced

Prepare the grill for cooking over direct medium heat. Lay the slices of lemon on both planks, covering them. Lay the shrimp in a single layer on 1 plank and the scallops on the other. Drizzle the shrimp and the scallops with the melted butter. In a small bowl, combine the salt, lemon pepper, paprika, garlic, and thyme. Sprinkle the mixture over both planks. Put the planks on the grill and cook until the shrimp and scallops are opaque, about 30 minutes. Remove the planks to a baking sheet or sheet of aluminum foil. Sprinkle the green onions over the top and serve right on the planks.

MAKES 6 SERVINGS

Dr. BBQ's Lobster with Chili-Lime Butter

This is the recipe I used in the Barbecue Championship Series to get my team to the semifinals. The lime and chili go very well with the lobster for something a little different. (Pictured on page 122.)

CHILI-LIME BUTTER

1 cup (8 ounces) butter

Juice of 2 limes

2 tablespoons good-quality chili powder

Salt, as needed

Black pepper, as needed

2 whole live Maine lobsters, about 1½ pounds each

Your favorite barbecue rub, as needed

Prepare the grill for cooking over direct medium heat. In a small saucepan, melt the butter and blend in the lime juice, chili powder, and salt and pepper to taste. Set aside.

Split the lobsters completely in half down the back with a chef's knife. Remove the tails and claws. Discard the rest. Crack the shells on the claws and inject or drizzle them each with 1 tablespoon of the butter. Season the tails lightly with the rub. Grill the tails and claws for about 5 minutes on each side. Spoon some of the Chili-Lime Butter into the tail shells. Cook until the lobster is just barely done, another 4 to 5 minutes. This will vary depending on your grill. Serve the remaining Chili-Lime Butter for dipping.

MAKES 2 SERVINGS

Houston Texans

HOME STADIUM

Two Reliant Park
Houston, TX 77054

CAPACITY

69,500

OFFICIAL WEB SITE

www.houstontexans.com

FIRST GAME PLAYED

September 8, 2002

CHAMPIONSHIPS

None

SIGNATURE FOOD OF THE AREA

Barbecue

GREAT BARBECUE

Thelma's Bar B Que

GREAT STEAKHOUSE

Vic and Anthony's Steakhouse

GREAT BREW

Shiner Bock

HALL OF FAMERS

None

CHEERLEADERS

Texans Cheerleaders

BEST SEASON

2007 (8–8)

HOUSTON AND FOOD

The city of Houston is all Texas. There are big buildings and big oil businesses and big pickup trucks and big hats everywhere. They eat beef because there's lots of it in Texas. Steaks and barbecued brisket are very popular here, but so is Mexican food. Mexico isn't very far away, and the climate is the same, so it's just natural. You'll see Mexican and Tex-Mex restaurants everywhere you look, with an occasional barbecue joint and a beer joint in between. Sometimes they're even the same place. You should also be able to find a good chicken-fried steak in Houston without looking too hard. It is considered by many to be the official dish of Texas. Don't forget the oysters and great seafood from the Gulf of Mexico either. There's a great selection of food in Houston.

Here are my suggestions for what to cook for a Texans Game-Day Party. Mix and match as you wish.

Sweet Sticky Barbecue Salsa (page 38) with chips

Grilled Chili-Rubbed Shrimp Cocktail (page 56)

Pozole (page 88)

Barbecued Brisket Sandwiches (page 109)

Spicy Spare Ribs (page 155)

Chipotle Pinto Beans (page 199)

Loaded Cornbread Casserole (page 208)

Chocolate-Apricot Tacos (page 224)

Fish Fry with Hush Puppies

A great way to feed a game-day crowd. Serve with coleslaw and beans.

FISH

1 cup buttermilk

1 large egg

2 cups cornflake crumbs

½ cup all-purpose flour

1½ teaspoons salt

¼ teaspoon black pepper

2 pounds boneless white fish fillets, cut into serving-size pieces

HUSH PUPPIES

2 cups cornmeal

2 tablespoons all-purpose flour

1 tablespoon baking powder

1 teaspoon baking soda

1 teaspoon salt

⅛ teaspoon cayenne

2 cups buttermilk

⅓ cup diced onion

2 jalapeños, finely chopped

1 large egg

2 cups vegetable oil

To make the fish: In a shallow dish, blend the buttermilk and egg. Combine the cornflake crumbs, flour, salt, and pepper on a plate or piece of waxed paper. Dip the fish into the egg mixture, then coat it with the crumb mixture. Put the breaded fish on waxed paper on a baking sheet in a single layer. When all the fish is breaded, refrigerate it for 30 minutes.

Meanwhile, to make the hush puppies: In a large bowl, mix the cornmeal, flour, baking powder, baking soda, salt, and cayenne. Add the buttermilk, onion, jalapeños, and egg. Mix thoroughly. In a large heavy skillet, heat the oil over medium-high heat until it reaches 350°F. Drop the batter by small round spoonfuls into the hot oil. Fry until they're golden brown and they float. Remove the hush puppies to paper towels to drain. Repeat with the remaining batter.

Add a few pieces of fish to the oil. Fry for 4 to 6 minutes on each side, or until golden. Repeat with the remaining fish. Place on a paper towel–lined plate to drain. Serve the fish and hush puppies while hot.

MAKES 6 SERVINGS

Tasty Salmon in a Package with Veggies

You can make the packages ahead and cook them at the game.

Cooking oil spray

1 small zucchini, julienned

1 yellow squash, julienned

1 medium carrot, julienned

1 clove garlic, crushed

Olive oil, as needed

Salt, as needed

Black pepper, as needed

Four 6-ounce fillets fresh salmon

1 medium tomato, seeded and diced

4 green onions, sliced

4 leaves fresh basil

1 lemon, thinly sliced

½ cup white wine

Preheat the oven to 400°F or prepare the grill for cooking over indirect medium-high heat. Lay out 4 double-thick sheets of heavy-duty aluminum foil 12 x 12 inches large. Spray the foil with cooking spray.

In a medium bowl, toss the zucchini, squash, carrot, and garlic together. Place one quarter of the mixture in the center of each piece of foil. Drizzle with oil and sprinkle lightly with salt and pepper. Lay a salmon fillet on top of each pile of vegetables. Sprinkle lightly with salt and pepper. Top each salmon fillet with tomato, green onions, a basil leaf, and 2 or 3 slices of lemon. As you close up each packet, add 2 tablespoons of the wine and seal the foil tightly.

At this point these can be refrigerated for up to 1 day and cooked at the party. When it's time, cook the packets on a baking sheet in the oven or directly on the grill for about 20 minutes, or until the salmon flakes. To serve, place each packet on a plate and tear open the top, remembering that there is hot liquid in the bottom.

MAKES 4 SERVINGS

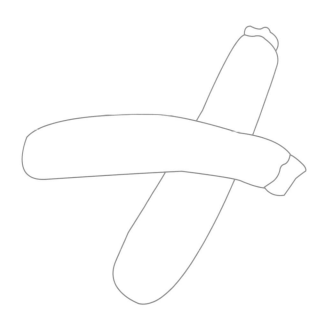

Greenbrier Smoked Peach Tea Chicken

One of my many jobs is teaching barbecue classes at The Greenbrier Resort in White Sulphur Springs, WV, along with my old friends Chris Lilly and Myron Mixon. The Greenbrier has a rich culinary history and I'm very proud to work with them. Chef Sue Moats, Chef Ken Hess, and April Pusey are the anchors of the program and we have all become good friends. I thank them and The Greenbrier for sharing this recipe. It's a good one.

GREENBRIER PEACH TEA RUB

⅓ cup ground peach tea
(such as Harney & Sons Loose Peach Tea)

8 teaspoons paprika

5 teaspoons sugar

5 teaspoons kosher salt

3 teaspoons ground black pepper

3 teaspoons granulated garlic

1½ teaspoons whole celery seed

⅛ teaspoon cayenne

⅛ teaspoon ground nutmeg

Pinch ground cinnamon

Pinch ground allspice

One 3 to 3½-pound frying chicken

2 tablespoons Greenbrier Peach Tea Rub

Greenbrier Peach Tea BBQ Sauce (facing page), as needed

To make the rub: Mix all the rub ingredients together. Store in an airtight container for up to 1 month. Makes about 1 cup.

Cut the whole chicken into 8 pieces. Season the chicken pieces on both sides with 2 tablespoons of the Peach Tea Rub (reserve the rest for another use). Refrigerate until needed.

Prepare the grill for cooking over indirect medium heat or preheat the smoker to 275°F, using hickory and apple wood for flavor. Place the chicken pieces directly on the grate, skin-side up. Close the smoker or grill and smoke until the chicken reaches an internal temperature of 165°F, about 1½ hours. Drizzle the sauce over or bathe the chicken in the sauce before serving.

MAKES 4 SERVINGS

Greenbrier Peach Tea BBQ Sauce

Greenbrier peach halves are available at The Greenbrier, but large frozen peach halves may be substituted.

2 Greenbrier peach halves, or large frozen peach halves, ¼ cup juice reserved

2½ cups water

⅓ cup ground peach tea (such as Harney & Sons Loose Peach Tea)

⅓ cup cider vinegar

2 tablespoons peach brandy (optional)

½ teaspoon granulated onion

½ teaspoon granulated garlic

¼ teaspoon celery salt

¼ teaspoon ground black pepper

2 cups mayonnaise

In a food processor, puree the peach halves with the peach juice and set aside. Bring the water to a boil in a small saucepot. Remove from the heat and add the peach tea. Allow it to steep for 30 minutes. Strain the tea through a coffee filter. Carefully squeeze the filter to remove all the concentrated tea.

In a medium saucepot, combine the prepared peach tea, peach puree, vinegar, brandy (if using), granulated onion, granulated garlic, salt, and pepper. Over medium heat, bring it to a simmer, stirring often. Remove from the heat and allow it to cool completely. Mix the cooled peach mixture with equal parts mayonnaise. If it is too thick, thin with more peach tea or peach juice. Refrigerate until needed.

MAKES ABOUT 1 QUART

NOTES

Greenbrier Peach Tea BBQ Sauce is like a butter sauce; it will break if heated. The sauce can be served cold or at room temperature.

This recipe was developed by Ethan Hileman, Sous Chef/Kitchen Manager of The Greenbrier; inspired by Big Bob Gibson's White Barbecue Sauce; and revised by inspired Chef Sue Moats of The Greenbrier Cooking School.

Barbecued Chicken Legs with Raspberry-Chipotle Barbecue Sauce

Chicken drumsticks are my favorite, not only for eating, but also for serving. A small plate or even just a napkin is all that's required for your guests. For these I've made a raspberry-chipotle sauce that's got a good kick to it and a great flavor.

12 chicken drumsticks

2 tablespoons olive oil

Your favorite barbecue rub, as needed

Wood chips (cherry or hickory preferred), soaked in water for 1 hour

Raspberry-Chipotle Barbecue Sauce (recipe follows)

Prepare the grill for cooking over direct medium heat. Rub the oil all over the chicken legs. Season the legs with the rub. Drain the wood chips and put them on top of the hot coals, or in the appropriate place for your grill. Put the chicken on the grill and close the lid to smoke them for 10 minutes. Continue cooking the chicken, turning often but reclosing the lid each time, for 40 minutes, or until the chicken reaches an internal temperature of 180°F. Brush the chicken with the sauce, flip, and brush again. Repeat this 2 or 3 times until the sauce is browned to your liking. Serve additional sauce on the side.

MAKES 12 SERVINGS

Raspberry-Chipotle Barbecue Sauce

The heat of this sauce can be adjusted by adding or subtracting a chipotle. Three works for me.

3 canned chipotles in adobo sauce, 1 tablespoon sauce reserved

1 cup seedless raspberry jam

½ cup ketchup

1 tablespoon freshly squeezed lemon juice

Pinch of salt

Add the chipotles to a blender. Top with the jam, ketchup, reserved adobo, lemon juice, and salt. Puree for 1 minute. Pour into a bowl to serve.

MAKES ABOUT 2 CUPS

Cream of Chicken Curry

A fiery and creamy dish that'll warm you up. The popularity of Thai food across the country has brought curry paste along with other great ingredients to the Asian aisle at most grocery stores.

One 3½-pound frying chicken, cut up

3 cups water

1 cube chicken bouillon (I like Knorr brand)

3 tablespoons olive oil

1 medium onion, chopped

1 large red bell pepper, chopped

2 stalks celery, chopped

1 serrano chile, chopped

One 11-ounce can condensed cream of chicken soup

1 cup milk

2 tablespoons yellow Thai curry paste

1 teaspoon lemon pepper

½ teaspoon salt

3 cups white rice, cooked

Put the chicken pieces in a Dutch oven and cover them with the water. It's okay if the chicken isn't fully submerged. Add the bouillon cube. Cover and place over medium-high heat. Bring to a boil and cook for 30 minutes. Turn the heat off and let the chicken rest, covered, for another 30 minutes.

Remove the chicken to a platter and set aside. Strain the cooking liquid and set aside. In a clean Dutch oven over medium heat, warm the oil. Add the onion, bell pepper, celery, and serrano and cook for about 5 minutes, until the onion is soft. Add the soup, milk, reserved cooking liquid, curry paste, lemon pepper, and salt. Bring to a simmer, cover, and cook for 20 minutes, stirring occasionally.

Meanwhile pull all the chicken meat from the bones into large pieces, discarding all the skin, cartilage, and bones. Add the chicken to the pot and cook for another 20 minutes, stirring occasionally but trying not to break the chicken up. Serve over hot rice.

MAKES 6 TO 8 SERVINGS

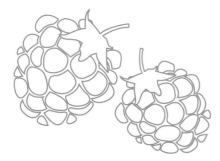

Jacksonville Jaguars

HOME STADIUM

Jacksonville Municipal Stadium
One Stadium Place
Jacksonville, FL 32202

CAPACITY

73,800

OFFICIAL WEB SITE

www.jaguars.com

FIRST GAME PLAYED

September 3, 1995

CHAMPIONSHIPS

None

SIGNATURE FOOD OF THE AREA

Fresh from the ocean

GREAT BARBECUE

Jenkin's Quality Barbecue

GREAT STEAKHOUSE

Plaza III

GREAT BREW

Gordon Biersch Blonde Bock

HALL OF FAMERS

None

CHEERLEADERS

The Roar

BEST SEASON

1999 (14–2)

JACKSONVILLE AND FOOD

Jacksonville is a big city but it's also a beach city. It sits very near the Atlantic Ocean in north Florida. Like any big city, there is access to all kinds of ingredients, and the beautiful high-end seaside resorts that are nearby surely create a market for all sorts of things. But the local fresh seafood is the great jewel of Jacksonville cuisine. It would be a shame to opt for anything but the ocean-fresh mahi mahi, the yellowfin ahi, or a beautiful local snapper when dining in Jacksonville. Opportunities like that only come along once in a while. If your plans are a little less uptown, remember that Florida is part of the South, so a good Southern meal is always close at hand. One of my favorite things in the South is the Krystal Burger. It's a little slider burger very similar to the White Castle of the North. You might want to try it when you're in Jacksonville as well.

Here are my suggestions for what to cook for a Jaguars Game-Day Party. Mix and match as you wish.

Dr. BBQ's Grilled Shrimp Toast (page 57)

Grilled Mahi Mahi Skewers with Peppered Bacon (page 59)

Homemade Tomato Soup (page 69)

Grilled Tuna Sandwiches with Chipotle Mayo (page 135)

Krystal Quiche (page 148)

Grilled Zucchini and Yellow Squash (page 199)

Peachy Sweet Potato Pie (page 203)

Key Lime Pie (page 214)

Game-Day Chicken and Baby Corn Stir-Fry

This is a fun and tasty stir-fry that can feed a big group.

MARINADE

¼ cup cornstarch

2 tablespoons peanut oil

2 tablespoons rice vinegar

1 tablespoon soy sauce

½ teaspoon white pepper

2 pounds boneless skinless chicken, cut into bite-size pieces (I prefer thighs but breasts will work)

Peanut oil, as needed (I keep mine in a 12-ounce plastic squeeze bottle)

1 medium onion, halved and sliced

3 stalks celery, sliced on a 45-degree angle

3 cloves garlic, thinly sliced

Two 8¾-ounce cans baby corncobs, drained and cut into thirds

1 cup diced fresh tomato

1 cup chicken broth

¼ cup oyster sauce

2 tablespoons soy sauce

½ teaspoon white pepper

½ cup water mixed with 1 tablespoon cornstarch

1 bunch green onions, cut on an angle into ½-inch pieces

Cooked, hot white rice, for serving

To make the marinade, in a medium glass bowl, whisk together the marinade ingredients. Add the chicken and toss well to coat. Refrigerate for at least 1 hour and up to 4 hours.

Preheat a very large wok. Squirt about ½ cup of peanut oil into the wok. Discard the marinade and add the chicken; cook for 2 minutes, stirring often and adding additional oil as needed. Push the chicken up the sides of the wok and squirt a couple more tablespoons of oil in the center. Add the onion, celery, and garlic and cook for 30 seconds, stirring them but keeping them in the center and separate from the chicken. Then stir everything together and mix well. Add the corn and tomato and mix well. Add the broth, oyster sauce, soy sauce, and pepper and mix well. Push everything to 1 side and add the water/cornstarch mixture to the juice in the bottom of the wok. Mix well and simmer until it begins to thicken. Toss everything together well and transfer the stir-fry to a large bowl. Top with the chopped green onions and serve with cooked, hot white rice.

MAKES 10 SERVINGS

TIPS FOR STIR-FRYING

When you are making a stir-fry, the cooking will go very quickly, so you have to prepare everything ahead of time and have it all lined up in bowls right by your cooking station. This is critical because there just won't be time to go in the house to get an ingredient without burning the dish.

The times and quantities in this recipe are for a very large 22-inch wok (see page 16) over a very hot outdoor burner. If you're doing this indoors and your wok isn't as big, you may have to do it in two batches and you'll have to adjust the cooking times.

Big Time Stir-Fry

This is my loaded version of a stir-fry, with lots of tasty ingredients.

MARINADE

¼ cup cornstarch

2 tablespoons peanut oil

2 tablespoons rice vinegar

1 tablespoon soy sauce

½ teaspoon white pepper

2 pounds pork tenderloin, cut into bite-sized pieces

Peanut oil, as needed (I keep mine in a 12-ounce plastic squeeze bottle)

1 medium onion, halved and sliced

1 green bell pepper, halved and sliced

3 cloves garlic, thinly sliced

2 serrano chiles, finely chopped

1 tablespoon finely chopped peeled fresh ginger

8 ounces sliced mushrooms

8 ounces medium, fresh shrimp, peeled and deveined

1 cup vegetable broth

3 tablespoons soy sauce

1 tablespoon sesame oil

1 tablespoon hoisin sauce

½ teaspoon white pepper

½ cup water mixed with 1 tablespoon cornstarch

1 bunch green onions, cut on an angle into ½-inch pieces

Cooked, hot white rice, for serving

To make the marinade, in a medium glass bowl, whisk together the marinade ingredients. Add the pork and toss well to coat. Refrigerate for at least 1 hour and up to 4 hours.

Preheat a very large wok. Squirt about ½ cup of peanut oil into the wok. Discard the marinade and add the pork; cook for 1 minute, stirring often and adding additional oil as needed. Push the pork up the sides of the wok and squirt a couple more tablespoons of oil in the center. Add the onion, bell pepper, garlic, chiles, and ginger and cook for 30 seconds, stirring them but keeping them in the center and separate from the pork. Then stir everything together and mix well. Add the mushrooms and shrimp and mix well. Cook for 1 minute, stirring often and adding more oil if needed. Add the broth, soy sauce, sesame oil, hoisin sauce, and white pepper and mix well. Push everything to 1 side and add the water/cornstarch mixture to the juice in the bottom of the wok. Mix well and simmer until it begins to thicken. Toss everything together well and transfer the stir-fry to a large bowl. Top with the chopped green onions and serve with cooked, hot white rice.

MAKES 12 SERVINGS

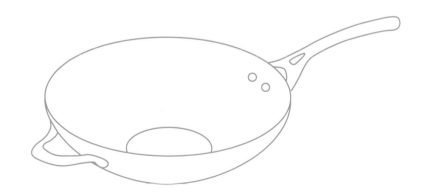

Scottie's Fried Turkey

This recipe comes from my friend Scottie Johnson. Scottie won the Jack Daniel's World Barbecue Championship in 2006. Scottie and his beautiful daughters, Zoe and Lexi, run the Corliss Johnson Memorial Foundation in memory of his wife and their mom, who left us way too early. You'll need a turkey fryer like I described on page 16 and the oil to go with it, plus a marinade injector. But fried turkey is a special treat that you'll find yourself making often. It's not just for Thanksgiving anymore!

SCOTTIE'S CREOLE BUTTER

2 cups (1 pound) butter

One 12-ounce can beer

1 tablespoon barbecue rub of your choice

1 tablespoon paprika

1 tablespoon freshly ground white pepper

1 tablespoon freshly and finely ground black pepper

1 tablespoon sea salt

1 tablespoon granulated garlic

1 tablespoon granulated onion

1 tablespoon dry mustard

1 teaspoon cayenne

One 15-pound turkey, fully defrosted

Seasoned salt, as needed

Peanut oil

For the injection, melt the butter in a small saucepan. Add the beer, rub, paprika, peppers, salt, garlic, onion, mustard, and cayenne. Mix well and remove from heat.

Remove all the giblets and the neck from the turkey and tuck the wings behind the neck. Using a kitchen injector, inject all of the marinade throughout the turkey, using small amounts in many different places. Season lightly inside and out with seasoned salt. Let the turkey rest at room temperature for 30 minutes.

Prepare the turkey fryer per the manufacturer's instructions. Add the peanut oil per the manufacturer's instructions for the proper fill level. Bring the temperature to 325°F. Gently drop the turkey into the oil. Return the temp to 325°F and hold it between there and 350°F for 3 minutes per pound, or until the internal temperature deep in the turkey thigh reaches 180°F. Remove the turkey to drain over newspaper and let it rest for 20 minutes. Carve and serve.

MAKES 12 SERVINGS

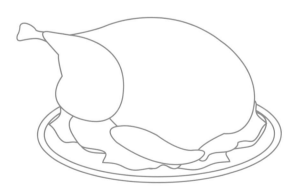

Baked Ziti with Garlic Bread

Kind of a better lasagna with the salami and meatballs inside.

3 tablespoons olive oil

1 medium onion, chopped

1 green bell pepper, chopped

5 cloves garlic, crushed

Two 28-ounce cans crushed tomatoes

1 pound dried ziti

20 premade mini meatballs

4 ounces salami, chopped

1 pound ricotta, softened

8 ounces sliced mozzarella

Garlic Bread (recipe follows)

Preheat the oven to 350°F. In a large saucepan over medium heat, warm the oil. When it's hot, add the onion and bell pepper and cook for 2 to 3 minutes. Add the garlic and cook for another 2 to 3 minutes, until the onions and bell pepper are soft. Add the tomatoes and bring to a simmer, stirring occasionally. Remove from the heat and set aside. Reserve 1 cup of this mixture in a separate bowl to be used as the topping.

Meanwhile, cook the ziti according to the package directions, being sure not to overcook it. A little on the chewy side is best because it will finish up when it's baked. Drain the ziti well and put it in a big bowl. Add the remaining sauce mixture and fold in. Let this cool for 10 minutes, tossing occasionally. Put half the ziti mix in a half hotel pan or 9-x-13-inch baking pan. Spread evenly. Top with an even layer of the meatballs, then the salami, then the ricotta, and then the rest of the ziti mixture. Top with the sliced mozzarella and then the reserved 1 cup of the sauce.

At this point the whole pan can be refrigerated for a day or two, well covered. If you're going to continue, cover it with foil and bake for 30 minutes. Remove the foil and cook for an additional 30 minutes, or until hot and bubbly. If you have refrigerated the ziti, you'll want to let it warm at room temperature for 1 hour first, then bake as directed. Serve hot with garlic bread.

MAKES ABOUT 15 SERVINGS

FILLING

½ cup (4 ounces) butter, softened

1 tablespoon granulated garlic

1 tablespoon paprika

2 teaspoons salt

2 teaspoons black pepper

2 teaspoons granulated onion

1 teaspoon dried basil

1 loaf Cuban or Italian bread, split and cut into thirds

Garlic Bread

Mix all the filling ingredients together well. Spread the filling on the cut sides of all the bread pieces. Put the halves back together and wrap each pair in a double layer of foil. Bake at 350°F for 20 minutes or grill for 5 minutes per side, until warm on the inside and crispy on the outside. Separate all the halves and cut each piece into 4.

MAKES 24 SERVINGS

Indianapolis Colts

1953–1983 Baltimore Colts,
1984–present Indianapolis Colts

HOME STADIUM

RCA Dome
200 South Capitol Avenue
Indianapolis, IN 46225

CAPACITY

60,272

OFFICIAL WEB SITE

www.colts.com

FIRST GAME PLAYED

September 27, 1953

CHAMPIONSHIPS

WFC Champions 1958, 1959,
1964, 1968

AFC Champions 1970, 2006

NFL Champions 1958, 1959, 1968

Super Bowl Champions 1970, 2006

SIGNATURE FOOD OF THE AREA

Breaded pork tenderloin

GREAT BARBECUE

Squealer's

GREAT STEAKHOUSE

St. Elmo Steak House

GREAT BREW

Oaken Barrel Indiana Amber

HALL OF FAMERS

Raymond Berry, End, 1955–1967

Eric Dickerson, RB, 1987–1991

Art Donovan, DT, 1950, 1953–1961

Weeb Ewbank, Coach, 1954–1962

Ted Hendricks, LB, 1969–1973

John Mackey, TE, 1963–1971

Gino Marchetti, DE, 1953–1964, 1966

Lenny Moore, F-RB, 1956–1967

Jim Parker, G-T, 1957–1967

Johnny Unitas, QB, 1956–1972

CHEERLEADERS

Colts Cheerleaders

BEST SEASON

1968 (13–1)

INDIANAPOLIS AND FOOD

Indianapolis is a big city in the middle of cornfields. Now that's not a bad thing. The corn that's grown around the city is great stuff and I'm happy to eat some anytime. The corn also feeds the hogs that grow around Indiana, and I sure think hogs are good. Some of that corn is famously made into popping corn for us too, and we all like that while we're watching a movie. So I'd say the food scene around Indianapolis is very much hearty Middle American with a downtown chef-driven scene thrown in. There's the very popular White Castle across from the Indianapolis Speedway, a place that tourists always remember about their visit to Indy, and last but not least is St. Elmo Steak House. It's a classic old downtown steakhouse with pictures of celebs and racecar drivers on the wall, and the steaks are first-class, but it's the shrimp cocktail there that will get you. The sauce is loaded with horseradish, and as a waiter once told me, "The last one is the hottest!"

Here are my suggestions for what to cook for a Colts Game-Day Party. Mix and match as you wish.

Wing Ding Dry Rub Wings (page 47)

Barbecued Chicken Nachos (page 52)

Pork and Rice Stew (page 89)

Barbecued Pulled Pork Sandwiches (page 108)

Mini Meat Loaves (page 161)

Grapes and Yogurt Salad (page 193)

Spicy Tangy Slaw (page 194)

Whiskey Girl's Caramel-Apple Pie (page 215)

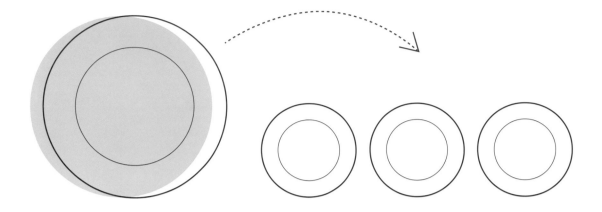

Special Side Dishes

No matter what main dishes you've chosen for your game-day feast, you're going to need some great side dishes to complete your meal.

The choices are endless and I've created some great recipes to get you started. For many guests, the side dishes make the meal. I know many people who go to a certain chicken place because the coleslaw is so good, and I know barbecue joints that are famous because their beans are so good.

I take great pride in dishes like my Peachy Sweet Potato Pie (page 203) and my Chipotle Pinto Beans (page 199). They are as good as any main dish and can even be the highlight of the meal. I also like to use side dishes to include something a little offbeat like Grilled Grits (page 208) or Grapes and Yogurt Salad (page 193). These are probably things most of the guests haven't had before, so it will make for good conversation, and of course they'll be asking you for the recipe.

You can also use the sides to cover all your bases. If you're serving a lot of meat you should consider a salad of some sort and possibly a fruit or veggie side, and a starch like potatoes or rice can fit in with just about any meal. The sides are the critical course to bring it all together and may even satisfy a light eater or a vegetarian that you didn't know about. I *am* Dr. BBQ and consider myself 100 percent carnivore, but there is a great satisfaction in pleasing a vegetarian. I may not get the concept but I think they should eat good food, too. So please don't just take the sides for granted or make the same easy thing all the time. Your game-day guests will thank you for it.

Cheesy Deviled Eggs

Cheese and bacon in a deviled egg sounds good to me.

12 large eggs

One 11-ounce can Cheddar cheese soup

4 slices bacon, cooked and crumbled

1 teaspoon good-quality chili powder

Pinch of salt

Paprika, for dusting

Place the eggs in a large saucepan and add enough cold water to cover them completely by 1 inch. Bring to a full boil over high heat. Once the water is brought to a full boil, reduce the heat to a medium boil. Cook for 10 minutes. Remove from the heat and immediately place the eggs under running cold water for 2 minutes. Transfer them to a bowl of ice water to chill completely.

When the eggs are completely chilled, peel and cut them in half lengthwise, reserving the yolks in a medium bowl and the whites on a serving platter or egg plate. Mash the yolks with a fork. Add the cheese soup, bacon, chili powder, and salt and mix well. Using 2 small spoons, fill each egg white with the filling. Dust with paprika and serve.

MAKES 24 SERVINGS

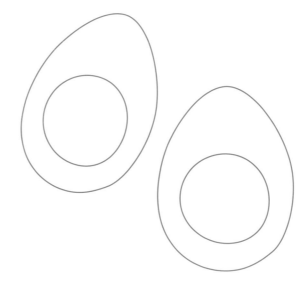

Chopped Garden Salad

A trendy salad that goes with everything.

DRESSING

²/₃ cup extra-virgin olive oil

¹/₃ cup balsamic vinegar

2 tablespoons freshly squeezed lemon juice

1 teaspoon celery salt

½ teaspoon white pepper

½ teaspoon dry mustard

¼ teaspoon granulated garlic

¼ teaspoon paprika

SALAD

3 cups chopped iceberg lettuce

3 cups chopped romaine lettuce

1 medium zucchini, thinly sliced

1 carrot, thinly sliced

½ cup chopped red cabbage

½ cup sliced radishes

1 medium cucumber, thinly sliced

½ cup sliced fresh mushrooms

2 green onions, thinly sliced

1 large ripe tomato, cubed

¼ cup (1 ounce) coarsely grated Swiss cheese

In a jar with a tight-fitting lid, combine the oil, vinegar, lemon juice, celery salt, pepper, mustard, garlic, and paprika. Shake vigorously to blend. Chill thoroughly.

In a large bowl, toss together the lettuces, zucchini, carrot, cabbage, radishes, cucumber, mushrooms, green onions, tomato, and cheese. Add half of the dressing and toss well. Add the remaining dressing as needed.

MAKES 10 SERVINGS

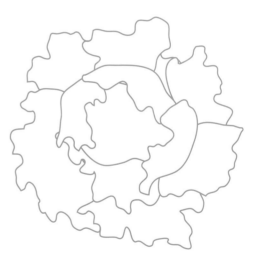

Game-Day Caesar Salad

Raw eggs are a food-safety no-no, especially at an outdoor party, so I've used cooked eggs for this salad. It's still got that great Caesar taste and texture.

3 large hard-boiled eggs, whites and yolks separated

4 cloves garlic, crushed

2 teaspoons anchovy paste

1 teaspoon Dijon mustard

2 tablespoons freshly squeezed lemon juice

1 tablespoon red wine vinegar

1 teaspoon Worcestershire sauce

½ cup extra-virgin olive oil

1 head romaine lettuce

1 cup croutons

½ cup (2 ounces) grated Parmesan cheese

Salt, as needed

Black pepper, as needed

In a small bowl, use a fork to mash together the egg yolks, garlic, anchovy paste, and mustard to a smooth paste. Add the lemon juice, vinegar, and Worcestershire. Mix thoroughly. Gradually add the oil, a little at a time, whisking constantly, until the dressing is emulsified. Transfer it to a jar with a tight-fitting lid. Refrigerate.

Wash, spin, and tear the lettuce into bite-size pieces. Place it in a zip-top bag and refrigerate.

When ready to serve, place the romaine in a large salad bowl, shake the dressing vigorously, pour it over the romaine, and toss. Chop the egg whites. Add the croutons and egg whites to the salad. Toss. Top with the cheese. Season with salt and pepper to taste.

MAKES 4 SERVINGS

Kansas City Chiefs

HOME STADIUM

Arrowhead Stadium
One Arrowhead Drive
Kansas City, MO 64129

CAPACITY

79,451

OFFICIAL WEB SITE

www.kcchiefs.com

FIRST GAME PLAYED

September 7, 1963

CHAMPIONSHIPS

AFL Champions 1966, 1969

Super Bowl Champions 1969

SIGNATURE FOOD OF THE AREA

Barbecue

GREAT BARBECUE

Oklahoma Joe's

GREAT STEAKHOUSE

Plaza III

GREAT BREW

Boulevard Pale Ale

HALL OF FAMERS

Marcus Allen, RB, 1993–1997
Bobby Bell, LB, 1963–1974
Buck Buchanan, DT, 1963–1975
Len Dawson, QB, 1962–1975
Lamar Hunt, Owner, 1960–2006
Willie Lanier, LB, 1967–1977
Marv Levy, Coach, 1978–1982
Joe Montana, QB, 1993–1994
Warren Moon, QB, 1999–2000
Jan Stenerud, PK, 1967–1979
Hank Stram, Coach, 1963–1974
Emmitt Thomas, DB, 1966–1978
Mike Webster, C, 1989–1990

CHEERLEADERS

Chiefs Cheerleaders

BEST SEASON

1968 (12–2)

KANSAS CITY AND FOOD

Kansas City is a town where almost everyone is willing to stay up all night cooking a barbecued brisket. They understand that it takes that long and they truly believe that their brisket is better than anyone else's, so it's worth the effort. That attitude has created the hottest barbecue cook-off scene anywhere in the country and the largest sanctioning body for cook-offs nationally, the Kansas City Barbeque Society. This is a big barbecue town. It's also a big steak town. There are at least half a dozen steakhouses in KC that would be the best one in town in some very big cities. It all began with the stockyards many years ago, and the tradition continues even though the stockyards are long gone. You can still find great butcher shops in KC, though, like Bichelmeyer's near the old stockyards. They've been doing it for three generations. This all translates to one of the wildest tailgating scenes in all of the NFL. The Chiefs' fans really know how to have a party.

Here are my suggestions for what to cook for a Chiefs Game-Day Party. Mix and match as you wish.

Wing Ding Dry Rub Wings (page 47)

Stuffed Jalapeños Wrapped in Bacon (page 63)

Big Pot Tailgate Chili (page 94)

Barbecued Brisket Sandwiches (page 109)

Woodford-Marinated Rib-Eye Steaks (page 163)

Barbecue Pit Beans (page 200)

Double-Baked Potatoes with Gorgonzola (page 201)

Loaded Brownies (page 221)

Lettuce and Tomato Wedges with Creamy Blue Cheese

The steakhouse classic moves to the parking lot.

4 ounces blue cheese, crumbled

1 cup mayonnaise

½ cup buttermilk

½ teaspoon granulated garlic

2 tablespoons minced chives

1 large head lettuce

2 large ripe tomatoes

To make the dressing, in a medium bowl, mash half of the cheese with ½ cup of the mayo until it is almost smooth. Gradually add the remaining mayo, the buttermilk, and garlic. Mix thoroughly, then add the remaining cheese and the chives. Cover and refrigerate for at least 30 minutes and up to 4 hours.

When ready to serve, cut the lettuce into 6 wedges and each tomato into 6 wedges. Place a lettuce wedge on a serving plate with 2 tomato wedges. Spoon the dressing over the lettuce and tomatoes.

MAKES 6 SERVINGS

¾ cup halved grape tomatoes

½ cup sliced black olives

½ cup thinly sliced red bell pepper

½ cup chopped green bell pepper

½ cup thinly sliced red onion

½ cup canned garbanzo beans, drained

½ cup thinly sliced salami, cut into strips

¼ cup grated carrot

¼ cup fresh basil leaves, sliced

½ teaspoon ground black pepper

6 cups cooked bow-tie pasta

1 cup Italian salad dressing

Salt, as needed

½ cup (2 ounces) grated Parmesan cheese

¼ cup chopped fresh parsley

Kitchen Sink Pasta Salad

A real crowd-pleaser that matches well with just about anything.

In a large bowl, toss together the tomatoes, olives, bell peppers, onion, beans, salami, carrot, basil, and pepper. Put the pasta in a large serving bowl and spread the vegetable mix over the pasta. Pour the salad dressing over the top. Toss gently until well mixed. Add salt as needed and mix again. Top with the cheese and parsley. Cover and refrigerate for 4 hours.

MAKES 12 SERVINGS

Grapes and Yogurt Salad

I had a similar dish at a barbecue party and just loved it, so I made a version of my own. You should mix the grapes with the dressing at the last minute or the dressing will break down and look bad.

1 cup vanilla yogurt

1 cup whipped topping (such as Cool Whip)

½ cup sour cream

4 ounces cream cheese, softened

⅓ cup packed brown sugar

3 cups halved seedless red grapes

3 cups halved seedless green grapes

In a large glass bowl, whisk together the yogurt, whipped topping, sour cream, cream cheese, and brown sugar. Reserve a few of each color of grapes for garnish. Right before serving, fold in the grapes gently until they are mixed in. Top with the reserved grapes and serve.

MAKES 10 SERVINGS

Hawaiian Fruit Salad

Everybody will have a scoop of this one.

2 cups fresh pineapple chunks

1 cup fresh cantaloupe chunks

1 cup fresh honeydew melon chunks

2 bananas, cut into ¼-inch slices

1 pound red seedless grapes, halved

1 pint strawberries, halved

1 cup mini marshmallows

Freshly grated zest, and juice of 1 lime

1 tablespoon honey

1 cup plain low-fat yogurt

1 cup whipped topping (such as Cool Whip)

½ cup sweetened coconut flakes

2 teaspoons vanilla extract

Fresh mint leaves, for garnish (optional)

In a large bowl, toss together the pineapple, cantaloupe, honeydew, bananas, grapes, strawberries, and marshmallows. Add the zest and lime juice. Drizzle the honey over the fruit and gently toss. Cover and refrigerate for 2 hours.

In a medium bowl, mix together the yogurt, whipped topping, coconut, and vanilla. Cover and refrigerate for 2 hours. When ready to serve, pour the yogurt mixture over the fruit. Fold the mixtures until well blended. Garnish with mint leaves, if desired.

MAKES 8 SERVINGS

Homemade Apple Slaw

A slaw that's a little different than most. This is especially good with any pork dish.

DRESSING

1 cup mayonnaise

⅓ cup freshly squeezed lemon juice

1 teaspoon sugar

One 1-pound package shredded coleslaw mix

1 large Granny Smith apple, cored and thinly sliced

¾ cup raisins

In a large bowl, mix together the dressing ingredients. Add the slaw mix, apple, and raisins. Toss to coat. Let rest for 5 minutes and toss again. Refrigerate for at least 4 hours and preferably overnight before serving.

MAKES 8 SERVINGS

Spicy Tangy Slaw

This slaw goes well with all the real barbecue dishes.

DRESSING

⅓ cup olive oil

¼ cup cider vinegar

½ teaspoon salt

½ teaspoon black pepper

½ teaspoon red pepper flakes

½ teaspoon sugar

One 1-pound package shredded coleslaw mix

½ red bell pepper, thinly sliced

½ medium onion, thinly sliced

1 jalapeño, halved and thinly sliced

In a large bowl, mix together the dressing ingredients. Add the slaw mix, bell pepper, onion, and jalapeño. Toss to coat. Let rest for 5 minutes and toss again. Refrigerate for at least 4 hours and preferably overnight before serving.

MAKES ABOUT 8 SERVINGS

Creamy Coleslaw

A great version of the classic slaw. I like to serve this one with the Barbecued Chicken Legs with Raspberry-Chipotle Barbecue Sauce (page 176).

DRESSING

2 cups mayonnaise

¼ cup cane syrup (such as Steen's, or substitute maple if you can't find cane syrup)

¼ cup powdered ranch dressing mix

1 teaspoon celery seed

One 1-pound package shredded cole-slaw mix

¾ cup dried pineapple, cut into small pieces

In a large bowl, mix together the dressing ingredients. Add the slaw mix and pineapple. Toss to coat. Let rest for 5 minutes and toss again. Refrigerate for at least 4 hours and preferably overnight before serving.

MAKES 8 SERVINGS

Warm German Potato Salad

My favorite type of potato salad, and it's safe for an outdoor party because there isn't any mayonnaise to worry about.

4 pounds russet potatoes

8 ounces bacon

½ cup all-purpose flour

1½ cups water

1 cup cider vinegar

½ cup sugar

1 teaspoon salt

¼ teaspoon black pepper

¾ cup chopped green onions

¾ cup chopped celery

¼ cup chopped fresh parsley

In a large stockpot, cook the whole potatoes in salted boiling water until fork tender. Drain, cool, peel, and slice the potatoes, about ½ inch thick. Set aside.

Cut the bacon into small pieces. In a large skillet, fry the bacon over medium-high heat until crisp. Remove it with a slotted spoon, and set aside on paper towels to drain. In the same skillet, reduce the heat to medium. Add the flour to the bacon drippings, and whisk until smooth. While whisking, add the water, vinegar, sugar, salt, and pepper. Whisk constantly until the dressing is thick and smooth, about 3 minutes. Add the potatoes, bacon, green onions, and celery. Toss gently until well mixed. Cook until heated through, about 5 minutes. Transfer to a serving dish and top with the parsley.

MAKES 8 SERVINGS

Miami Dolphins

HOME STADIUM

Dolphin Stadium
2269 Dan Marino Boulevard
Miami Gardens, FL 33056

CAPACITY

74,916

OFFICIAL WEB SITE

www.miamidolphins.com

FIRST GAME PLAYED

September 2, 1966

CHAMPIONSHIPS

AFL/AFC Champions 1971, 1972,
1973, 1982, 1984

Super Bowl Champions 1972, 1973

SIGNATURE FOOD OF THE AREA

Cuban

GREAT BARBECUE

Shorty's BBQ

GREAT STEAKHOUSE

Shula's

GREAT BREW

Have a mojito instead

HALL OF FAMERS

Nick Buoniconti, LB, 1969–1976
Larry Csonka, FB, 1968–1974, 1979
Bob Griese, QB, 1967–1980
Jim Langer, C, 1970–1979
Larry Little, G, 1969–1980
Dan Marino, QB, 1983–1999
Don Shula, Coach, 1970–1995
Dwight Stephenson, C, 1980–1987
Thurman Thomas, RB, 2000
Paul Warfield, WR, 1970–1974

CHEERLEADERS

Dolphins Cheerleaders

BEST SEASON

1972 (14–0)

MIAMI AND FOOD

Miami just might be one of the best dining cities anywhere. There is all the fresh seafood you could ever want, and chefs make great use of it. Grouper and mahi mahi and snapper dominate the menus. Then there's the huge Cuban influence that not only supports the authentic Cuban restaurants but also brings all those great ingredients to the market for all the high-flying chefs to use. Restaurants like Nobu, Norman's, and Prime 112 are serving world-class cuisine in Miami and the crowds are loving it. Miami is all about the beach too. There aren't many better food events than the South Beach Wine and Food Festival, held early each year right on the beach. Sit in an alfresco café on Ocean Drive and sip a mojito, dine on the freshest seafood in the world, and watch the beautiful people walk by. Miami is a great place to be.

Here are my suggestions for what to cook for a Dolphins Game-Day Party. Mix and match as you wish.

Banana-Nut Bread (page 34)

Grilled Chili-Rubbed Shrimp Cocktail (page 56)

Spicy Black Bean Soup (page 82)

Catfish Tacos with Citrus Salsa (page 134)

Ray's Tropical Pork Chop Sandwiches (page 140)

Grapes and Yogurt Salad (page 193)

Grilled Zucchini and Yellow Squash (page 199)

Citrus Flan (page 226)

"Just Can It" Bean Salad

It doesn't get any easier or tastier than this.

One 15-ounce can cannellini beans, rinsed and drained

One 15-ounce can dark red kidney beans, rinsed and drained

One 15-ounce can black beans, rinsed and drained

One 15-ounce can lima beans, rinsed and drained

One 15-ounce can artichoke hearts, rinsed and drained

½ cup olive oil

⅓ cup balsamic vinegar

3 tablespoons soy sauce

2 tablespoons chopped pimiento

2 tablespoons capers, rinsed and drained

1 teaspoon dried basil

½ teaspoon black pepper

½ cup (2 ounces) grated Parmesan cheese

In a large bowl, combine all the ingredients except the cheese. Mix gently, cover, and refrigerate for 2 hours. When ready to serve, toss again and top with the cheese.

MAKES 10 SERVINGS

Grilled Zucchini and Yellow Squash

Simple, attractive, and delicious.

⅓ cup olive oil

⅓ cup balsamic vinegar

1 tablespoon honey

1 tablespoon salt

1 tablespoon black pepper

1 tablespoon dried basil

1 tablespoon dried oregano

2 cloves garlic, crushed

3 yellow crookneck squash

3 medium zucchini

In a medium bowl, whisk together the oil, vinegar, honey, salt, pepper, basil, oregano, and garlic. Wash the squash and zucchini and halve them lengthwise. Place them in a zip-top bag and pour the marinade over them. Push out as much air as possible and seal the bag. Refrigerate for at least 2 hours and preferably overnight.

Prepare the grill for cooking over direct high heat. Remove the squash and zucchini from the bag and place them directly on the grill, skin-side down. Discard the marinade. Cook for 5 minutes and flip over. Cook another 5 minutes, or until the squash and zucchini are browned and softened. Remove to a cutting board and cut into bite-size pieces. Mix together in a bowl to serve.

MAKES 6 SERVINGS

Chipotle Pinto Beans

Cooking dried beans is a little bit more trouble than canned beans, but they taste completely different. This recipe is definitely worth the effort.

4 slices bacon

1 small onion, chopped

1 clove garlic, crushed

3 canned chipotles in adobo sauce, chopped

1 pound dried pinto beans, soaked in cold water for 4 hours

3 cups water

2 cups strong coffee

¼ cup packed brown sugar

2 teaspoons ground cumin

1 teaspoon salt

1 cube beef bouillon (I like Knorr brand)

In a Dutch oven over medium heat, cook the bacon until crisp. Remove the bacon to drain on paper towels and add the onion. Add a little vegetable oil if needed. Cook the onion for 3 minutes, then add the garlic and chipotles. Continue cooking, stirring often, until the onion is soft.

Drain the beans. Add the beans, water, coffee, sugar, cumin, salt, and bouillon to the pot. Crumble the bacon and add it. Stir well and bring to a boil. Reduce to a simmer. Cover and cook for 2 hours, stirring occasionally and adding a little water if needed, until the beans are tender.

MAKES 12 SERVINGS

Barbecue Pit Beans

These are the classic barbecue-joint beans. They go with everything and everyone loves them.

4 slices bacon

2 tablespoons butter

1 medium onion, chopped

1 green bell pepper, chopped

1 jalapeño, finely chopped

One 55-ounce can baked beans, extra liquid poured off

1 cup packed brown sugar

1 cup of your favorite barbecue sauce

¼ cup yellow mustard

2 tablespoons of your favorite barbecue rub

Preheat the smoker to 300°F or prepare the grill for cooking over indirect medium-low heat, using apple or hickory wood for flavor.

In a medium skillet over medium-high heat, cook the bacon until crisp. Remove the bacon to drain on paper towels. Add the butter to the skillet. Add the onion, bell pepper, and jalapeño and cook until the onion is soft, about 5 minutes. Remove from the heat. Crumble the bacon and set aside. In a large bowl, combine the beans, brown sugar, sauce, mustard, rub, the reserved bacon, and the reserved onion mixture. Mix well. Transfer to a 13-x-9-inch aluminum-foil pan. Cook in the smoker or grill, uncovered for 2 hours, until hot and bubbly.

MAKES 10 SERVINGS

Zesty Roasted Garlic Mashed Potatoes

A modern-day classic. These are great with any of the steak dishes. If you're traveling with these, simply add another ⅓ cup of half-and-half so they will stay soft.

5 pounds russet potatoes

⅓ cup sour cream

⅓ cup half-and-half

¼ cup (2 ounces) butter

1 head roasted garlic (see page 160), squeezed from the skin

2 teaspoons salt

1 teaspoon red pepper flakes

½ teaspoon ground black pepper

Peel and quarter the potatoes. In a large pot, cover the potatoes with cold water. Cook over medium-high heat for 30 minutes, or until the potatoes are fork tender. Drain the potatoes and leave them in the pot. With a handheld potato masher, mash the potatoes, adding the sour cream, half-and-half, butter, garlic, salt, pepper flakes, and pepper. Mash and mix until the potatoes are light and fluffy. Transfer to a serving dish.

MAKES 8 SERVINGS

Double-Baked Potatoes with Gorgonzola

Cheesy and delicious.

4 large russet potatoes

4 ounces crumbled Gorgonzola cheese

¼ cup sour cream

¼ cup half-and-half

2 tablespoons butter

½ teaspoon salt

¼ teaspoon black pepper

Preheat the oven to 400°F.

Scrub the potatoes, and pierce them with a fork several times. Bake the potatoes on a baking sheet for 55 minutes, or until soft to the touch. Remove them to cool for 30 minutes.

Cut a slice off the top of each potato. With a spoon, scoop out the potato pulp into a medium bowl, leaving a thin layer inside of the potato shell. With a handheld masher, mash the potato pulp with the cheese, sour cream, half-and-half, and butter. Add the salt and pepper, and mix thoroughly. Heap the mixture back into the potato shells, put them on a baking sheet, and return to the oven. Bake for 15 minutes, or until hot.

MAKES 4 SERVINGS

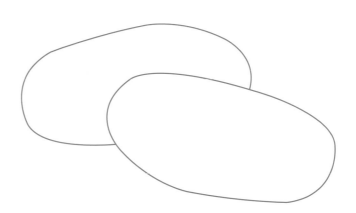

Nancy P.'s Smoked Cheddar Double-Baked Potatoes

I was at my friend Nancy's house one day and I tricked her into making these and writing down the recipe for me. They're really good. (Pictured on page 127.)

4 large baking potatoes

1 tablespoon vegetable oil

5 tablespoons butter

2 bunches green onions, white and light green parts only, chopped

4 cloves garlic, crushed

2 tablespoons heavy cream

1 teaspoon salt

½ teaspoon black pepper

1 cup ½-inch cubes smoked Cheddar cheese

Paprika, as needed

Preheat the oven to 350°F.

Wash the potatoes, poke a few holes in them, and rub them with the oil. Bake for 1 hour, or until tender. Let them cool for 30 minutes.

Meanwhile in a small skillet over medium heat, melt the butter. Add the onions and garlic and cook for 2 to 3 minutes, until the onions are soft. Set aside. Slice the top off the potatoes and scoop out the pulp into a medium bowl. Set the skins aside. With a potato masher, crush the potato pulp. Add the onion mixture, cream, salt, and pepper and mix well. Add the cheese and fold gently until mixed well. Spoon the potato mixture back into the shells. Sprinkle lightly with paprika. Put the potatoes on a baking sheet and return to the oven for 15 minutes, or until hot.

MAKES 4 SERVINGS

Peachy Sweet Potato Pie

I make this dish on a regular basis when I take my turn cooking for the guests at the Hubbard House in Orlando. It's a great and worthy place that my friend Maurice Barnlund brought into my life and I thank him for that. The guests have loved ones in critical care and Hubbard House takes wonderful care of them. I only wish I could help them more often.

2 large sweet potatoes

⅓ cup butter, at room temperature

⅓ cup sugar

⅔ cup evaporated milk

⅓ cup peach preserves

2 large eggs, lightly beaten

½ teaspoon vanilla extract

½ teaspoon salt

2 unbaked 9-inch pie shells

Peel and cube the sweet potatoes. Put them in a large saucepan and cover with salted cold water. Bring to a simmer and cook until they are soft, about 5 minutes. Drain, mash, and set aside to cool a bit. Preheat the oven to 350°F.

In a large bowl, beat together the butter and sugar until creamy. Add in the milk, preserves, eggs, vanilla, and salt. Mix well. Add the sweet potatoes and whisk until well blended. Pour the mixture into the pie shells and put them in the oven. Cook for about 45 minutes, or until a knife inserted in the middle comes out clean.

Allow the pies to cool, and serve at room temperature.

MAKES 16 SERVINGS

New England Patriots

HOME STADIUM

Gillette Stadium
One Patriot Place
Foxboro, MA 02035

CAPACITY

68,756

OFFICIAL WEB SITE

www.patriots.com

FIRST GAME PLAYED

September 9, 1960

CHAMPIONSHIPS

AFC Champions 1985, 1996, 2001, 2003, 2004, 2007

Super Bowl Champions 2001, 2003, 2004

SIGNATURE FOOD OF THE AREA

Baked beans

GREAT BARBECUE

Blue Ribbon BBQ

GREAT STEAKHOUSE

The Oak Room

GREAT BREW

Samuel Adams Boston Lager

HALL OF FAMERS

Nick Buoniconti, LB, 1962–1968
John Hannah, G, 1973–1985
Mike Haynes, CB, 1976–1982
Andre Tippett, LB, 1982–1993

CHEERLEADERS

Patriots Cheerleaders

BEST SEASON

2007 (16–0)

BOSTON AND FOOD

Any city that is nicknamed "Beantown" is probably going to have good food. Durgin-Park, a Boston restaurant landmark, says on their Web site that they were established before you were born. They also offer an authentic Boston baked bean recipe and another for Indian pudding. Those are old food traditions in Boston. This was also the longtime home of Julia Child. How's that for credentials? They love baked beans and boiled dinners, but Boston is also a major seaport, so you'll see lots of fresh fishcakes and chowdah and lobstah rolls. It's all great stuff and real Boston history. Maybe that's why Julia moved there. Boston is also the home of celebrity chefs like Todd English, Ming Tsai, and my culinary brother Dirty Dick Westhaver. Dick is a great chef and a better barbecue cook. Don't miss the wonderful old Italian restaurants in Boston and the many traditional Irish pubs. They might even have some good food there.

Here are my suggestions for what to cook for a Patriots Game-Day Party. Mix and match as you wish.

Baked Brie with Chutney and Crisp Bacon (page 43)

Three-Bean Nachos (page 53)

Smoky Beef Stew (page 84)

Turkey Gravy Sandwiches with Homemade Cranberry Sauce (page 138)

Plank-Cooked Shrimp and Scallops (page 169)

Zesty Roasted Garlic Mashed Potatoes (page 200)

Barbecue Pit Beans (page 200)

White-Bottom Pumpkin Pie (page 213)

BBQ-Rubbed Fruit Kabobs

I've chosen the fruits that are my favorite to grill, but you can substitute just about anything. Choose what you like and what is in season. (Pictured on page 126.)

4 kiwi, each sliced into 3 thick slabs

3 peaches, quartered and pitted

12 big chunks of fresh pineapple

6 long bamboo skewers, soaked in water for 1 hour

Dr. BBQ's Fruit Rub (recipe follows)

Prepare the grill for cooking over direct medium-high heat. Thread 2 pieces of each fruit onto a skewer, alternating them. Be sure to skewer the kiwi through the side so the cut face is showing. Sprinkle all sides liberally with Dr. BBQ's Fruit Rub.

Place the kabobs directly on the grill and cook for 3 to 4 minutes on each side, or until golden brown.

MAKES 6 SERVINGS

Dr. BBQ's Fruit Rub

¼ cup packed brown sugar

¼ cup white sugar

1 tablespoon good-quality chili powder

1 tablespoon lemon pepper

1 teaspoon salt

1 teaspoon ground nutmeg

½ teaspoon ground cinnamon

¼ teaspoon cayenne (optional)

In a small bowl, mix together all the ingredients. Store them in a sealed container at room temperature for up to 3 months.

MAKES ¾ CUP

Parking Lot Pork Fried Rice

I've been in search of a great fried rice recipe to make at home for many years. My friend Chef Ray Tang once told me the secret ingredient that I was missing was BTUs and that if my wok got hot enough my fried rice would be good. I believed him but there wasn't much I could do about it until now. Read about the Big Kahuna Wok Kit on page 16 and you'll see what I'm using now to make great fried rice.

¾ cup peanut oil

½ cup soy sauce

1 teaspoon sesame oil

½ teaspoon white pepper

6 large eggs, lightly beaten

3 cups small-dice cooked pork (grilled or smoked is best)

1 cup green onions cut on an angle and 1 inch long

6 cups cold cooked rice

2 cups bean sprouts

Put the oil in a squeeze bottle for easy access. In a small bowl, combine the soy sauce, sesame oil, and pepper. Set aside.

Heat the wok until it's very hot. Squirt ¼ cup of the peanut oil into the wok. Add the eggs and stir-fry them, breaking them up until they're cooked through. Remove the eggs from the wok. Squirt a little more of the oil into the wok and add the pork and green onions. Cook for 30 seconds, stirring often. Add another ¼ cup of oil and then the rice. Stir often, breaking up the rice and moving everything around. Continue cooking for about 2 minutes, or until the rice begins to brown. Add the soy sauce mixture and continue cooking and stirring. Add the rest of the peanut oil, the eggs, and bean sprouts. Continue stirring until everything is mixed well and hot. Remove from the wok and serve.

MAKES 8 SERVINGS

TIPS FOR STIR-FRYING

When you are making a stir-fry, the cooking will go very quickly, so you have to prepare everything ahead of time and have it all lined up in bowls right by your cooking station. This is critical because there just won't be time to go in the house to get an ingredient without burning the dish.

The times and quantities in this recipe are for a very large 22-inch wok (see page 16) over a very hot outdoor burner. If you're doing this indoors and your wok isn't as big, you may have to do it in two batches and you'll have to adjust the cooking times.

Grilled Grits

Most grits are one of those things that are just a little something extra on your plate, but these are pretty special and they won't fall through the grates if you make them like this!

Quick grits, enough for 12 servings

2 cups (8 ounces) grated Cheddar cheese

One 4-ounce can diced mild green chiles

¼ cup (2 ounces) butter, cut into pieces

1 tablespoon salt

1 tablespoon black pepper

1 tablespoon paprika, plus extra as needed

1 tablespoon sugar

Butter a 9-x-13-inch baking dish.

Prepare the grits per the package directions. Remove them from the heat and add in the cheese, chiles, butter, salt, pepper, paprika, and sugar. Mix until well blended. Spread the grits evenly in the baking pan and smooth the top. Cover with plastic wrap. Let cool for 30 minutes, then refrigerate for at least 4 hours and preferably overnight.

When you're ready to serve them, prepare the grill for cooking over direct high heat. Cut the grits into 20 squares and dust them on the top and bottom with additional paprika. Grill them for 2 to 3 minutes per side, just until they warm up and get a little color. If you cook them too long, they'll fall apart. Gently take them off the grill and serve.

MAKES 20 SERVINGS

Loaded Cornbread Casserole

It's part cornbread, part casserole, and all good.

1¼ cups yellow cornmeal

1 teaspoon baking powder

1 teaspoon salt

½ teaspoon baking soda

1 cup milk

½ cup (4 ounces) butter, melted

4 large eggs, lightly beaten

Two 15-ounce cans creamed corn

1 cup (4 ounces) shredded Cheddar cheese

6 slices bacon, cooked and crumbled

1 cup french-fried onions (from the can)

Preheat the oven to 350°F. Grease a 9-x-13-inch pan.

In a big bowl, combine the cornmeal, baking powder, salt, and baking soda. Add the milk, butter, and eggs. Mix well. Add the corn and mix well. Pour into the prepared pan. Spread the cheese and bacon evenly over the top. With a fork, push the cheese and bacon into the batter, just submerging it. Sprinkle the onions over the top. Bake for about 1 hour, until a toothpick inserted comes out clean. Serve warm or at room temperature.

MAKES 15 SERVINGS

Baked Macaroni and Cheese

The classic that goes well with any grilled food.

1 pound dried elbow macaroni

¼ cup (2 ounces) butter

¼ cup all-purpose flour

½ teaspoon granulated garlic

½ teaspoon granulated onion

½ teaspoon salt

¼ teaspoon black pepper

2 cups milk

2 cups (8 ounces) grated Cheddar cheese

¾ cup dried bread crumbs

Preheat the oven to 400°F.

Cook the macaroni as directed on the package. Drain. Transfer it to a greased 2-quart casserole dish. Set aside.

In a small saucepan over medium heat, melt the butter, then whisk in the flour, garlic, onion, salt, and pepper. Gradually blend in the milk, stirring often. Cook and stir until the mixture thickens and bubbles. Stir in the cheese, and mix until smooth. Remove from the heat. Pour the cheese sauce over the macaroni and toss well. Sprinkle the top with the bread crumbs. Bake for 15 minutes, or until bubbly.

MAKES 8 SERVINGS

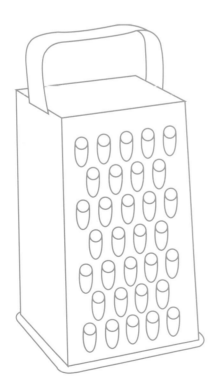

New York Jets

HOME STADIUM

Giants Stadium
East Rutherford, NJ 07073

CAPACITY

79,469

OFFICIAL WEB SITE

www.newyorkjets.com

FIRST GAME PLAYED

September 11, 1960

CHAMPIONSHIPS

AFL Champions 1968

Super Bowl Champions 1968

SIGNATURE FOOD OF THE AREA

Hot Dogs

GREAT BARBECUE

Southern Hospitality

GREAT STEAKHOUSE

Robert's Steakhouse

GREAT BREW

Brooklyn Brewery

HALL OF FAMERS

Weeb Ewbank, Coach, 1963–1973
Ronnie Lott, S, 1994
Don Maynard, WR, 1960–1972
Art Monk, WR, 1994
Joe Namath, QB, 1965–1976
John Riggins, RB, 1971–1975

CHEERLEADERS

None

BEST SEASON

1968 (11–3)

NEW YORK AND FOOD

You can see my thoughts on New York (page 77), but the menu here is a little different. Although they hail from the same city, the fans of the Jets are said to be a little more excitable than the fans of that other New York team, so I've selected my menu accordingly.

Here are my suggestions for what to cook for a Jets Game-Day Party. Mix and match as you wish.

Asian Orange Wings (page 51)

Dr. BBQ's Grilled Shrimp Toast (page 57)

Homemade Tomato Soup (page 69)

Steak Sandwiches on Garlic Bread with Grilled Onions (page 110)

Peachy Baby Back Ribs (page 154)

Chopped Garden Salad (page 188)

Homemade Apple Slaw (page 194)

Harvey Wallbanger Cake (page 218)

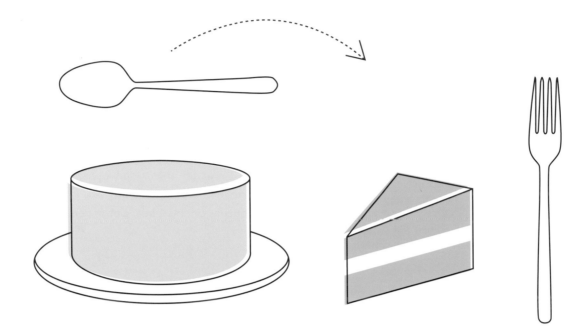

GREAT FINISHES:

Fabulous Desserts

Someone once famously said that life is uncertain and you should eat dessert first. I wouldn't normally agree with that, and I don't think I've ever done it, but I've noticed that when the cookies or brownies get put out early on game day, they begin to disappear early too. I'm no food cop, so I say let them eat cake, or brownies, or pie. If it makes my guests happy, then I'm happy.

This matches up very well with my thinking that you should make sure to put some food out early to keep the natives from becoming restless while you're preparing the main courses, and it also goes along with my thought that you should serve many dishes for grazing throughout the day. It's a long game day. There are a few appetizers in the beginning of this book that look suspiciously like desserts anyway, such as Sticky Fingers Cinnamon Bread (page 34) and Banana-Nut Bread (page 34), so you can sneak one of those in if you really want to save your special dessert for later. Or, you can use some of the more flexible desserts as appetizers, such as Sweet Blueberry-Apricot Crumble (page 227) or Doenee's Nutella Bars (page 219), and you can sneak the Peachy Sweet Potato Pie (page 203) from the side dish chapter in anywhere.

So let's sort this out. You could serve a sweet appetizer and some cookies early, use the sweet potato pie as a side dish, and finish with a cake and another pie, and you'd have worked five desserts into your menu. I know some people who would think that was a very good game-day spread.

Trish Trigg's Pecan Pie

This recipe deserves an encore. Over the years this pecan pie recipe has probably won more dessert awards at barbecue cook-offs around the country than any other one dish. When you try it you'll understand why. (Pictured on page 128.)

1 cup sugar

1 cup light corn syrup

3 large eggs, lightly beaten

2 tablespoons butter, at room temperature

1 teaspoon vanilla extract

1¼ cups whole pecans

1 unbaked 9-inch pie shell

Preheat the oven to 350°F.

In a large bowl, whisk together the sugar, syrup, eggs, butter, and vanilla until well blended. Stir in the pecans. Pour the mixture into the pie shell. Bake for 50 to 55 minutes, or until set. Let it cool completely on a wire rack before serving.

MAKES 8 SERVINGS

White-Bottom Pumpkin Pie

The white chocolate chips are a tasty addition to this pumpkin pie.

1 unbaked deep-dish 9-inch pie shell

One 15-ounce can pure pumpkin

One 12-ounce can evaporated milk

2 large eggs, lightly beaten

½ cup packed brown sugar

¼ cup granulated sugar

1 tablespoon pumpkin pie spice

½ teaspoon salt

1 cup white chocolate chips

Whipped cream, for garnish

Preheat the oven to 350°F.

Poke holes all over the bottom of the pie crust. Bake it by itself for 10 minutes. Set aside to cool.

In a large bowl, combine the pumpkin, milk, eggs, sugars, spice, and salt. Mix well. Spread the white chocolate chips evenly on the bottom of the pie shell. Pour the pumpkin mixture over the top. Bake for about 55 minutes, or until a toothpick inserted in the middle comes out clean. Remove to a rack to cool completely, about 2 hours. Slice and serve with whipped cream.

MAKES 8 SERVINGS

Key Lime Pie

This is a simple and delicious Key lime pie. It's the official pie of Florida and a favorite everywhere else. You probably won't be able to get fresh Key limes and the regular limes aren't the same, so look for bottled Key lime juice at the grocery store or order it online.

3 large egg yolks

One 14-ounce can sweetened condensed milk

½ cup Key lime juice

1 prebaked 9-inch graham cracker pie shell

Whipped cream, for garnish

Preheat the oven to 350°F.

Beat the egg yolks and milk in a medium bowl with a mixer at high speed until light and fluffy, about 5 minutes. Add the lime juice and mix well. Pour the mixture into the shell. Bake for 20 minutes, or until set. Let the pie cool completely. Garnish with whipped cream to serve.

MAKES 8 SERVINGS

Whiskey Girl's Caramel-Apple Pie

This recipe comes from my friend Marsha Russell from Lynchburg, Tennessee. I always ask Marsha to share a recipe for my books and, little by little, I'm getting all of her good ones.

CRUMB TOPPING

1 cup packed brown sugar

½ cup all-purpose flour

½ cup quick-cooking oats

½ cup (4 ounces) butter

½ cup granulated sugar

3 tablespoons all-purpose flour

1 teaspoon ground cinnamon

⅛ teaspoon salt

6 cups peeled and thinly sliced cooking apples

1 unbaked deep-dish 9-inch pie shell

CARAMEL TOPPING

½ cup store-bought caramel topping

1 tablespoon butter

2 tablespoons Jack Daniel's whiskey

½ cup chopped pecans

Preheat the oven to 375°F.

Make the crumb topping by stirring together the brown sugar, flour, and oats in a medium bowl. Cut in the butter until the topping turns into crumbs. Set aside.

In a large bowl, stir together the sugar, flour, cinnamon, and salt. Add the apple slices and toss until coated. Pour the apple mixture into the pie shell.

Sprinkle the crumb topping over the apple mixture. Place the pie on a cookie sheet to catch the drippings. Cover the edge of the shell with aluminum foil. Bake for 20 minutes. Remove the foil and bake for 30 minutes more, or until the topping is golden brown.

When the pie comes out of the oven, make the caramel topping by combining the caramel and butter in a small saucepan. Cook over medium heat, stirring often until the butter melts and mixes well with the caramel sauce. Remove from the heat and stir in the whiskey. Sprinkle the pie with the chopped pecans, and drizzle it with the caramel sauce. Cool on a wire rack. Serve warm or at room temperature.

MAKES 8 SERVINGS

Oakland Raiders

HOME STADIUM

McAfee Coliseum
7000 Coliseum Way
Oakland, CA 94621

CAPACITY

63,146

OFFICIAL WEB SITE

www.raiders.com

FIRST GAME PLAYED

September 11, 1960

CHAMPIONSHIPS

AFL/AFC Champions 1967, 1976, 1980, 1983, 2002

Super Bowl Champions 1976, 1980, 1983

SIGNATURE FOOD OF THE AREA

Tri-tip

GREAT BARBECUE

Everett and Jones BBQ

GREAT STEAKHOUSE

Kincaid's

GREAT BREW

Blue Whale Ale

HALL OF FAMERS

Marcus Allen, RB, 1982–1992
Fred Bilentnikoff, WR, 1965–1978
George Blanda, PK/QB, 1967–1975
Bob Brown, T, 1971–1973
Willie Brown, CB, 1967–1978
Dave Casper, TE, 1974–1980, 1984
Al Davis, Owner, 1963–present
Eric Dickerson, RB, 1992
Mike Haynes, CB, 1983–1989
Ted Hendricks, LB, 1975–1983
James Lofton, WR, 1987–1988
Howie Long, DE, 1981–1993
Ronnie Lott, S, 1991–1992
John Madden, Coach, 1969–1978
Ron Mix, OT, 1971
Jim Otto, C, 1960–1974
Art Shell, G, 1968–1982
Gene Upshaw, G, 1967–1981

CHEERLEADERS

Raiderettes

BEST SEASON

1967 & 1976 (13–1)

OAKLAND AND FOOD

It may be right across the bay from San Francisco, but the football team and the food in Oakland are very different. Oakland doesn't have the touristy seafood restaurants or the cable cars. It's a little grittier Northern California type of cuisine, just like the Raiders are a little grittier than the 49ers. The dish the people in Northern California like to eat more than anything else is grilled beef tri-tip, and Oakland is no exception. I've lived in Chicago and now Florida and rarely even see tri-tip in the grocery case at home, but in California the cases are full of them. It supposedly all started in Santa Maria, which is down the road a ways from the Bay Area, but it's spread now and the folks in Oakland are eating it up.

Here are my suggestions for what to cook for a Raiders Game-Day Party. Mix and match as you wish.

Grilled Avocado Halves (page 42)

Stuffed Jalapeños Wrapped in Bacon (page 63)

Spicy Black Bean Soup (page 82)

Fresh Breakfast Burritos (page 102)

Garlic-Grilled Tri-Tip (page 167)

Grapes and Yogurt Salad (page 193)

Double-Baked Potatoes with Gorgonzola (page 201)

Pear Cobbler with Raisins (page 219)

Harvey Wallbanger Cake

This recipe, based on the potent drink that was so popular in the 1980s, comes from my Big Green Egghead friends, Kevin and Tammy Jacques. They cook on the barbecue circuit as the Grilling Room and they do very well.

½ cup Galliano liqueur, divided

2 ounces mandarin orange vodka, divided

1½ cups freshly squeezed orange juice, divided

1 box orange cake mix (18½ ounces)

One 3.4-ounce box instant vanilla pudding mix

1 pint sour cream

½ cup vegetable oil

3 large eggs, lightly beaten

One 8.4-ounce can mandarin orange slices, drained and chopped

Whipped cream, for garnish

Preheat the oven to 350°F. Grease and flour a 10-inch Bundt pan.

In each of 2 separate large glasses, pour ¼ cup of the Galliano, 1 ounce of the vodka, and ¾ cup of the orange juice. Put ice in 1 of the glasses, stir, and drink it. Set the other glass aside.

In a large bowl, combine the cake mix, pudding mix, sour cream, oil, and eggs. Add the reserved cocktail to the mixing bowl. Beat with an electric mixer until smooth. Gently fold the oranges into the batter. Pour the batter evenly into the Bundt pan. Bake for 50 to 55 minutes, or until a toothpick inserted into the center comes out clean. Let the cake cool in the pan for 10 minutes, then remove it to a rack to cool completely. Garnish with whipped cream to serve.

MAKES 10 SERVINGS

Dried Cherry and Vanilla Bread Pudding

Make this ahead, then cool, slice, and take to the game for easy serving.

1 quart heavy cream

1 cup sugar

6 large eggs, lightly beaten

1 tablespoon vanilla extract

10 cups cubed day-old Cuban or French bread, not too crusty

2 cups dried cherries

½ cup crushed macadamia nuts

⅓ cup white chocolate chips

Preheat the oven to 350°F. Lightly grease a 9-x-13-inch baking pan.

In a bowl, combine the cream, sugar, eggs, and vanilla and mix well. Put the bread cubes in a big bowl. Pour the egg mixture over them and fold in until the bread is wet. Let it rest a few minutes and fold again. Pour the mixture into the greased baking pan. Use a spoon to spread the mixture evenly throughout the pan. Sprinkle with the cherries, nuts, and white chocolate chips. Using a spoon, push them into the pudding until they are mixed in but near the top. Bake for about 1 hour, or until set in the middle.

MAKES 12 SERVINGS

Pear Cobbler with Raisins

This is a great way to use pears in a dish that everyone loves.

COBBLER TOPPING

1½ cups all-purpose flour

⅓ cup sugar

1 tablespoon baking powder

½ teaspoon salt

½ cup (4 ounces) unsalted butter

½ cup half-and-half

1½ cups water

1 cup raisins

¾ cup sugar

3 tablespoons cornstarch

½ teaspoon ground cinnamon

¼ teaspoon salt

⅛ teaspoon ground cloves

6 medium Bartlett pears

To make the topping, in a large bowl, mix together the flour, sugar, baking powder, and salt. Cut in the butter until the mixture is crumbly. Add the half-and-half, and stir gently until the dough leaves the side of the bowl.

Preheat the oven to 400°F. Over medium-high heat in a 3-quart saucepan, combine the water, raisins, sugar, cornstarch, cinnamon, salt, and cloves. Heat the mixture to boiling, stirring constantly. Pour the mixture into a 9-x-13-inch baking dish.

Wash, peel, and core the pears. Slice them lengthwise to ½ inch thick. Arrange them on top of the raisin mixture. Crumble the topping over the pears. Bake for 25 to 30 minutes, until the topping is golden and the fruit mixture is hot and bubbly. Let rest for 10 minutes before serving.

MAKES 10 SERVINGS

Doenee's Nutella Bars

Doenee is my sister. Her real name is Denise, but when we were very young I couldn't say Denise, so I mumbled "Doenee" when I called her, and the name stuck. This is her recipe and it's great game-day food. By the way, Doenee is older than I am. (Pictured on page 125.)

1 cup light corn syrup

1 cup sugar

1 cup Nutella (chocolate-hazelnut spread)

6 cups crisp rice cereal

Lightly grease a 9-x-13-inch pan. In a Dutch oven over medium heat, cook the corn syrup, sugar, and Nutella, stirring often until the sugar is melted. Remove from the heat and add the cereal. Toss well, coating all of the cereal. Transfer the mixture to the pan and push down to form an even layer in the pan. Let cool for 30 minutes and cut into 20 bars.

MAKES 20 BARS

Barbara Lowe's Cook-Off Orange Bars

This recipe makes one of my favorite dishes to eat. Anytime the Firehouse BBQ team is at a cook-off, I look them up, and the "Team Mom" is sure to serve me a couple of these.

2 cups granulated sugar

1½ cups all-purpose flour

1 teaspoon salt

1 cup (8 ounces) unsalted butter, at room temperature

4 large eggs

2 teaspoons pure orange extract

2 teaspoons freshly grated orange zest

GLAZE

1 cup confectioners' sugar

2 tablespoons orange juice

2 teaspoons freshly grated orange zest

Preheat the oven to 350°F. Grease a 9-x-13-inch pan with a nonstick cooking spray and set aside.

In a medium bowl, stir together the granulated sugar, flour, and salt. Add the butter, eggs, orange extract, and zest and beat with an electric mixer until well blended. Pour the batter into the prepared pan and bake for 30 minutes, or until light golden brown. Remove from the oven and immediately pierce the top of the entire cake with a fork.

To make the glaze, combine the confectioners' sugar, orange juice, and additional zest in a medium bowl, stirring until smooth. Spread the glaze evenly over the cake while it is still hot. Cool the cake and cut into squares.

MAKES 24 SERVINGS

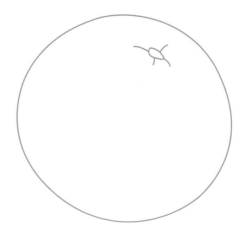
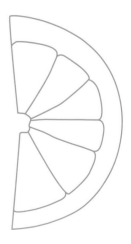

Loaded Brownies

If brownies are better with one added treat, they'll be better with four added treats.

1 cup sugar

½ cup (4 ounces) butter, at room temperature

3 large eggs, lightly beaten

1 cup all-purpose flour

¾ cup chocolate syrup

⅓ cup chopped walnuts

⅓ cup shredded sweetened coconut

⅓ cup mini chocolate chips

1 teaspoon vanilla extract

Preheat the oven to 350°F. Grease and lightly flour a 9-inch square baking pan.

In a large bowl, beat together the sugar, butter, and eggs until well blended. Stir in the flour, chocolate syrup, walnuts, coconut, chocolate chips, and vanilla. Combine thoroughly. Turn the batter into the greased baking pan. Bake for 40 minutes, or until the center is firm. Cool on a wire rack. Cut into 16 squares.

MAKES 16 SERVINGS

White Chocolate–Granola–Macadamia Cookies

The white chocolate and macadamia nuts go very well together in these cookies.

6 tablespoons (3 ounces) unsalted butter

½ cup packed brown sugar

1 large egg

1 cup all-purpose flour

1 cup granola

1 tablespoon ground cinnamon

1 teaspoon ground ginger

½ teaspoon baking soda

⅛ teaspoon salt

⅔ cup white chocolate chips

½ cup chopped macadamia nuts

Preheat the oven to 375°F. Lightly spray 2 nonstick cookie sheets with baking spray.

In a large bowl, beat the butter and sugar together. Beat in the egg. In another large bowl, combine the flour, granola, cinnamon, ginger, baking soda, and salt. Stir the dry ingredients into the butter mixture, and then add the white chocolate chips and macadamia nuts. Combine well. Drop from a teaspoon onto the prepared cookie sheets, spacing them about 2 inches apart. Bake for 8 to 10 minutes, or until browned. Remove from the sheets and cool on racks.

MAKES 36 SERVINGS

Pittsburgh Steelers

HOME STADIUM

Heinz Field
100 Art Rooney Avenue
Pittsburgh, PA 15212

CAPACITY

64,450

OFFICIAL WEB SITE

www.steelers.com

FIRST GAME PLAYED

September 20, 1933

CHAMPIONSHIPS

AFC Champions 1974, 1975, 1978, 1979, 1995, 2005

Super Bowl Champions 1974, 1975, 1978, 1979, 2005

SIGNATURE FOOD OF THE AREA

Primanti Brothers sandwiches

GREAT BARBECUE

Wilson's Bar-B-Q

GREAT STEAKHOUSE

The Coal Hill Steakhouse

GREAT BREW

Church Brew Pipe Organ Pale Ale

HALL OF FAMERS

Bert Bell, President, 1941–1946
Mel Blount, CB, 1970–1983
Terry Bradshaw, QB, 1970–1983
Len Dawson, QB, 1957–1959
Bill Dudley, RB, 1942, 1945–1946
Mean Joe Greene, DT, 1969–1981
Jack Ham, LB, 1971–1982
Franco Harris, RB, 1972–1983
Cal Hubbard, OT, 1936
John Henry Johnson, RB, 1960–1965
Walt Kiesling, Coach, 1939–1940,
1941–1944, 1954–1956
Jack Lambert, LB, 1974–1984
Bobby Layne, QB, 1958–1962
John McNally, Coach, 1934,
1937–1939
Marion Motley, RB, 1955
Chuck Noll, Coach, 1969–1991
Art Rooney, Owner, 1933–1988
Dan Rooney, Owner, 1955–Present
John Stallworth, WR, 1974–1987
Ernie Stautner, DT, 1950–1963
Lynn Swann, WR, 1974–1982
Mike Webster, C, 1974–1988

CHEERLEADERS

None

BEST SEASON

1967 & 1976 (13–1)

PITTSBURGH AND FOOD

Pittsburgh is one of the great American industrial cities and the food reflects that. The people who immigrated there to work many years ago brought the traditions and cuisines of their homelands with them, resulting in the many great ethnic restaurants and neighborhoods that still exist there. They love their old traditions and they love their Steelers. One of the favorite foods of Pittsburgh involves a big deli sandwich with the French fries piled high right on the sandwich. This sounds like a city that likes to eat. When I go there I head right to one of the Primanti Brothers sandwich shops and get the trip started with a capicola and cheese sandwich. It's a fine tradition and a fine sandwich.

Here are my suggestions for what to cook for a Steelers Game-Day Party. Mix and match as you wish.

Sticky Fingers Cinnamon Bread (page 34)

Wing Ding Dry Rub Wings (page 47)

Mac and Cheese Soup (page 74)

Steak Sandwiches on Garlic Bread with Grilled Onions (page 110)

Baked Ziti with Garlic Bread (page 183)

Game-Day Caesar Salad (page 189)

Grilled Zucchini and Yellow Squash (page 199)

Doenee's Nutella Bars (page 219)

Chocolate Chip–Mint Cookies

Put these out early and your guests will be very happy.

6 tablespoons (3 ounces) butter, at room temperature

½ cup packed dark brown sugar

1 large egg, lightly beaten

½ teaspoon vanilla extract

½ teaspoon mint extract

¾ cup all-purpose flour

¾ cup toasted wheat germ

½ teaspoon baking powder

1 cup chocolate chips

Preheat the oven to 350°F. Lightly grease a nonstick cookie sheet.

In a large bowl, beat the butter and sugar together. Beat in the egg, vanilla, and mint extract. In a separate bowl, combine the flour, wheat germ, and baking powder. Stir the flour mixture into the butter mixture. Add the chocolate chips and combine thoroughly. Drop rounded tablespoon-fuls of batter onto the cookie sheet, spacing them about 2 inches apart. Bake for 10 to 12 minutes, or until brown. Remove from the baking sheet to cool on a wire rack. Repeat until all the cookies are done.

MAKES 24 SERVINGS

Chocolate-Apricot Tacos

These may seem a little weird, but once you serve them your guests will want them again.

6 ounces spreadable cream cheese, at room temperature

¼ cup confectioners' sugar

½ teaspoon vanilla extract

Eight 6-inch flour tortillas

1 cup semisweet chocolate chips

16 dried apricots, cut into small pieces

16 vanilla wafers

Prepare the grill for cooking over direct medium heat, or preheat a frying pan over medium heat.

In a small bowl, mix together the cream cheese, sugar, and vanilla. Spread a thin layer of this mixture on 1 side of all the tortillas. Sprinkle the chocolate chips on one half of each of the tortillas, distributing them evenly among them. Sprinkle the apricots on the opposite side of the chocolate chips, distributing them evenly among the 8 tortillas. Place the vanilla wafers in a zip-top bag and crush them with the bottom of a sauce-pan. Sprinkle them over all the tortillas. Then fold the tortillas in half. Cook the tacos for 1 or 2 minutes on each side, just until warm.

MAKES 8 SERVINGS

Snickers-Stuffed Baked Apples

I needed a special recipe for a competition among grill companies in 2006, so I came up with these. I cooked them on the Big Green Egg and won the contest that day. I think those judges are still talking about them.

8 large Jonagold or other cooking apples

¼ cup (2 ounces) butter, at room temperature

¼ cup packed brown sugar

8 mini Snickers bars

8 large marshmallows

8 pecan halves

Freshly grated zest of 1 lemon

Preheat the oven to 350°F or prepare a grill for cooking over indirect medium heat.

With the large end of a melon baller, remove the stem and core of the apples, leaving the bottoms intact. Hollow the apples out so a Snickers bar and a marshmallow will fit inside each one. With a razor knife, score the skin of the apple from top to bottom every ½ inch. Then score a ring around the bottom of the apple to connect all of the top-to-bottom cuts. Rub the outsides of the apples with the butter and sprinkle with the brown sugar.

Place the apples in a greased pan. Place a Snickers bar in the cavity of each apple. Bake for 25 minutes. Add a marshmallow to the cavity of each apple. Bake for another 20 minutes, or until the apples are tender. Remove from the oven and top each apple with a pecan half and a little of the lemon zest.

MAKES 8 SERVINGS

Citrus Flan

A fresh twist on a wonderful classic.

CARAMEL

1½ cups sugar

2 tablespoons freshly squeezed lemon juice

2 tablespoons freshly squeezed lime juice

2 tablespoons freshly squeezed orange juice

CUSTARD

⅔ cup sugar

3 large eggs

3 large egg yolks

3 cups half-and-half

Freshly grated zest of 1 lemon

Freshly grated zest of 1 lime

Freshly grated zest of 1 orange

1 teaspoon vanilla extract

½ teaspoon salt

Preheat the oven to 350°F. Fill a 9-x-13-inch pan one-third of the way with water and put it in the oven.

In a medium saucepan, combine the sugar and the 3 juices for the caramel. Without stirring, cook over medium heat until the caramel is dark golden brown. This should take about 5 minutes. You want the sugar to get dark, but if it burns you'll need to start over. Pour the caramel into a 2-quart casserole with sloping sides. Tilt the casserole around to get the caramel as far up the sides as you can. Set aside.

In the bowl of a mixer, beat the sugar, eggs, and yolks on low speed until well blended. Add the rest of the ingredients and mix until well blended. Pour the egg mixture into the casserole. Place the casserole in the pan of water and cook for 1 hour and 15 minutes, or until set. Remove from the oven and cool for 30 minutes. Refrigerate for at least 4 hours and preferably overnight.

Loosen the sides with a knife. Place a serving platter over the flan and flip the casserole to transfer the flan to the platter. Spoon any loose caramel over the flan. There will be some hardened caramel that won't come out, but that's OK.

MAKES 8 SERVINGS

Sweet Blueberry-Apricot Crumble

The blueberries and apricots go beautifully together for this sweet dish.

3 pounds fresh apricots, pitted and quartered (peaches may be substituted)

1 cup granulated sugar

2 tablespoons freshly squeezed lemon juice

2 tablespoons quick-cooking tapioca

2 cups blueberries, fresh or frozen

1 cup all-purpose flour

^{2}/$_3$ cup packed brown sugar

1 teaspoon ground cinnamon

½ cup (4 ounces) cold butter

Ice cream or whipped topping, for garnish

Preheat the oven to 375°F. Lightly butter a 3-quart shallow baking dish.

In a large bowl, thoroughly combine the apricots, granulated sugar, lemon juice, and tapioca. Turn the mixture into the baking dish. Spoon the blueberries over the top. In a separate large bowl, combine the flour, brown sugar, and cinnamon. Cut in the butter until the mixture is crumbly. Sprinkle it over the fruit. Bake for 45 minutes, or until the apricots are tender and the crumb topping is browned. Cool at least 15 minutes before serving. Serve with ice cream or whipped topping.

MAKES 8 SERVINGS

San Diego Chargers

HOME STADIUM

Qualcomm Stadium
9449 Friars Road
San Diego, CA 92108

CAPACITY

71,500

OFFICIAL WEB SITE

www.chargers.com

FIRST GAME PLAYED

September 10, 1961

CHAMPIONSHIPS

AFL/AFC Champions 1963, 1994

SIGNATURE FOOD OF THE AREA

Mexican

GREAT BARBECUE

Real Texas BBQ

GREAT STEAKHOUSE

Greystone Steakhouse

GREAT BREW

AleSmith X

HALL OF FAMERS

Lance Alworth, WR, 1962–1970
Fred Dean, DE, 1975–1981
Dan Fouts, QB, 1973–1987
Sid Gillman, Coach, 1961–1969, 1971
Charlie Joiner, WR, 1976–1986
Deacon Jones, DE, 1972–1973
Larry Little, G, 1967–1968
John Mackey, TE, 1972
Ron Mix, OT, 1961–1969
Johnny Unitas, QB, 1973
Kellen Winslow, TE, 1979–1987

CHEERLEADERS

Charger Girls

BEST SEASON

2006 (14–2)

SAN DIEGO AND FOOD

It shouldn't be a surprise that the people of San Diego like Mexican food. Heck—they live right by the Mexican border. In the land of beautiful weather, the people spend much of their time outdoors, so their favorite foods are almost all game-day-friendly. Tacos and burritos are the main food groups in San Diego and the fish taco has become the favorite. Of course, they're also situated right on the ocean, so that's no surprise either. The fiery flavors of Mexican food coupled with the fresh fish make for a great combination. Eating a fish taco in the perfect San Diego weather with an ocean view is one of the great pleasures in life.

Here are my suggestions for what to cook for a Chargers Game-Day Party. Mix and match as you wish.

Grilled Avocado Halves (page 42)

Nachos Ai Chihuahua (page 53)

Pozole (page 88)

Catfish Tacos with Citrus Salsa
(page 134)

Gringo Huevos Rancheros (page 147)

Chopped Garden Salad (page 188)

Chipotle Pinto Beans (page 199)

Citrus Flan (page 226)

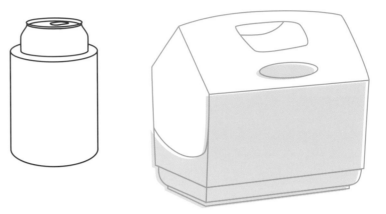

Delicious Drinks

A cooler of beer is at the center of many game-day parties, along with a cooler full of soft drinks, a few wine coolers, and some bottled water. These are the staples and should always be served on game day. Be sure to get a couple of beer choices—one of them nonalcoholic—and some diet and regular sodas. Many of us like to drink out of glass bottles and they are fine at home, but cans or plastic bottles are the only choice if you're in the parking lot because even one broken bottle can create a dangerous situation there.

If you're serving in those big, red plastic cups, make sure to have a magic marker on hand so the guests can personalize their cups. This will eliminate a lot of half-empty cups and lost drinks. Another staple on game day is coffee. It can warm you up and wake you up on a long, cold day. A big thermos is a must. I prefer regular old coffee, but I know some of my guests like that foo-foo flavored coffee, so I usually have some of both on hand.

I like to also add another game-day drink option. Sometimes it'll be as simple as a few bottles of wine or champagne or a couple bottles of flavored schnapps. But other times I like to feature a specialty drink for the occasion. The drinks in this chapter are great examples of what I like to serve. It's quite an eclectic collection. Feel free to mix and match them as you wish. The Real Southern-Style Sweet Tea (facing page) and Homemade Lemonade (facing page) can be combined in equal parts to make an Arnold Palmer. (Yes, he really does drink that.) The Homemade Lemonade goes well with a shot of vodka, and you can add a little hot sauce or horseradish to the Bloody Doctor (page 232) if that's your thing. Other than the Sweet Tea and the Homemade Lemonade, these are grown-up drinks meant only for the nondriving adults. Please serve them and enjoy them responsibly.

Real Southern-Style Sweet Tea

Making sweet tea is a serious thing in the southern United States. Up north, what you get is iced tea and you have to add sugar packets that don't dissolve. In the South, the waitress will be sure to keep your big glass full, and the tea is already loaded with real sugar and it's all dissolved. Here's how I like to make mine. If you're a real Southerner, you may want to up the sugar to 2 full cups.

1 gallon water, divided

4 family-size tea bags (designed to make 1 quart each)

1½ cups sugar

Ice cubes

In a medium saucepan, bring 1 quart of the water to a full boil. Remove it from the heat and drop in the tea bags. Let the tea steep for 6 minutes, tumbling the tea bags a couple times. Remove the tea bags and stir in the sugar. Let the tea rest for 1 minute and stir again until the sugar is all dissolved. Pour into a 1-gallon pitcher and add 1 more quart of water. Stir well. Add 1 or 2 trays of ice and stir again. Add enough water to fill the pitcher and stir again. Keep in the refrigerator and serve over ice.

MAKES 1 GALLON

Homemade Lemonade

It's so much better than the powdered stuff.

1½ cups water

1½ cups sugar

2 cups freshly squeezed lemon juice

2 quarts cold water

Ice cubes

In a small saucepan over medium heat, mix together the 1½ cups of water and the sugar. Cook and stir until the sugar melts and mixes with the water. Set aside to cool. In a 1-gallon pitcher, mix the sugar water (simple syrup), lemon juice, and 2 quarts of cold water. Mix well. Add ice to fill the pitcher and mix well.

MAKES 1 GALLON

Bistouille

When I was young my mom would often take us to visit the French relatives. If it was early in the day, the men would all be drinking a Bistouille. Sadly, the old French relatives were gone before I was old enough to appreciate the tradition that I was seeing.

8 ounces hot coffee

2 tablespoons sugar

1 ounce brandy

In a large mug, mix the coffee and the sugar well. Add the brandy and mix again.

MAKES 1 SERVING

The Bloody Doctor

Here is a barbecue man's version of the classic. (Pictured on page 115.)

End Zone Barbecue Rub (page 20), as needed

¼ fresh lemon

Ice cubes

2 ounces vodka

6 ounces chilled tomato juice

2 ounces your favorite barbecue sauce

Celery stick, for garnish

1 cooked jumbo shrimp, for garnish

Lay the rub on a saucer large enough for rimming the glass. Wet the rim of a large glass with the lemon (discard when lemon is done). Dip the rim in the rub. Fill the glass two-thirds of the way with ice. Add the vodka, tomato juice, barbecue sauce, and the juice from the ¼ lemon. Mix well. Put the celery stick in the glass and hang the shrimp on the rim.

MAKES 1 SERVING

Mr. Lampe's Summer Drink

This may sound crazy, but it was my dad's favorite summer drink. It's actually very good and I drink it often, but I still can't figure out why he only drank it in the summer.

Ice cubes

1½ ounces good-quality gin

8 ounces cola

Fill a large glass two-thirds of the way with ice. Add the gin and cola and mix well.

MAKES 1 SERVING

Chocolate Martini

I'm usually kind of a purist, but this is very good. (Pictured on page 123.)

Ice cubes

2 ounces vanilla vodka

2 ounces chocolate liqueur

Orange slice, for garnish

Fill a cocktail shaker two-thirds of the way with ice. Add the vodka and liqueur. Cover and shake well for 30 seconds. Strain into a martini glass. Garnish by hanging a slit orange slice on the rim of the glass.

MAKES 1 SERVING

Slow Woody

My friend Mark Williams is the executive chef at Brown-Foreman in Louisville and he's also a big supporter of the Slow Food movement in Kentucky. When he asked me to attend and speak to the guests at a Slow Food event at the Woodford Reserve distillery in Lexington, I was happy to oblige. For the occasion Mark created this drink and everyone enjoyed it, so I'm happy to include it here.

Ice cubes

2 ounces Woodford Reserve Kentucky Bourbon

8 ounces lemonade

1 ounce Tuaca Italian liqueur

Fill a large glass two-thirds of the way with ice. Add the bourbon and the lemonade. Mix well. Gently pour the Tuaca over the back of a spoon to make it float on top.

MAKES 1 SERVING

Tennessee Titans

1960–1996 Houston Oilers,
1997–1998 Tennessee Oilers,
1999–present Tennessee Titans

HOME STADIUM

LP Field
1 Titans Way
Nashville, TN 37219

CAPACITY

68,798

OFFICIAL WEB SITE

www.titansonline.com

FIRST GAME PLAYED

September 11, 1960

CHAMPIONSHIPS

AFL Champions 1960, 1961

AFC Champions 1999

SIGNATURE FOOD OF THE AREA

Southern

GREAT BARBECUE

Paradise Ridge Grille

GREAT STEAKHOUSE

The Stock Yard Restaurant

GREAT BREW

Yazoo Beer

HALL OF FAMERS

Elvin Bethea, DE, 1968–1983

George Blanda, QB-K, 1960–1966

Earl Campbell, RB, 1978–1984

Ken Houston, S, 1967–1972

Bruce Matthews, C, 1983–2001

Warren Moon, QB, 1984–1993

Mike Munchak, G, 1982–1993

CHEERLEADERS

Tennessee Titans Cheerleaders

BEST SEASON

1999 & 2000 (13–3)

NASHVILLE AND FOOD

It may be a big grown-up city, but Nashville sits right smack in the middle of Tennessee, where the nicest people in the world reside. Drive a half hour in any direction and you'll meet some fine country folks. So even though there are some trendy restaurants in Nashville now, the favorite cuisine is still down-home Southern cooking. Fried catfish, chicken and dumplings, biscuits and gravy, and grits are the foods that make everyone happy around there. They love their barbecue too, and you can find some wonderful old places that serve it very well. If you're really adventurous, there is a dish that's served in Nashville called "hot chicken." It's a specialty in a few restaurants and it is really spicy. If you don't like food that's super hot, don't even try it. I'll stick with the chicken and dumplings, and the best I've found are at the Paradise Ridge Grille in west Nashville. They also have the best barbecue in Nashville, so go hungry and try some of both.

Here are my suggestions for what to cook for a Titans Game-Day Party. Mix and match as you wish.

Sweet Potato Bread with Pecans (page 37)

Barbecued Chicken Nachos (page 52)

Dr. BBQ's Grandma's Chicken Dumpling Soup (page 70)

Barbecued Bologna Sandwiches (page 110)

Fish Fry with Hush Puppies (page 172)

Cheesy Deviled Eggs (page 187)

Grilled Grits (page 208)

Whiskey Girl's Caramel-Apple Pie (page 215)

Key Lime Margarita

A high-quality version of the original.

Lime slice, for garnish

Kosher salt

Ice cubes

2 ounces tequila, 100% agave recommended

1½ ounces Cointreau

1 ounce Key lime juice (Fresh squeezed is best, but Key limes are rare and the bottled juice isn't bad. Look for it in the grocery store or buy it online.)

Pinch of sugar

Rub the rim of a margarita glass with the lime and rim it with salt. Fill the glass halfway with ice. Fill a cocktail shaker two-thirds of the way with ice. Add the tequila, Cointreau, lime juice, and sugar. Shake vigorously for 30 seconds. Strain into the prepared glass. Garnish by cutting a slit into the lime slice and hanging it on the rim of the glass.

MAKES 1 SERVING

Dirty Dicktail

This recipe comes from my friend Richard "Dirty Dick" Westhaver. It's powerful!

Ice cubes

3 ounces good rum

3 ounces Mike's Hard Limeade

Cran-peach juice, as needed

1 lime wedge

1 slice orange

Fill a large glass with ice. Add the rum and limeade. Stir well. Top off with cran-peach juice and stir again. Garnish with a wedge of lime and a slice of orange.

MAKES 1 SERVING

Parking Lot Punch

This is a big drink for a big crowd and a big celebration.

One 8-pound bag of ice

1 gallon orange juice

1 gallon pineapple juice

1.75 liters dark rum

1.75 liters coconut rum

1 liter spiced rum

1 quart lemon juice

16 ounces grenadine

Add everything to a 5-gallon water cooler. Mix well. Serve over additional ice.

MAKES 40 SERVINGS

INDEX

TABLE OF EQUIVALENTS

The exact equivalents in the following table have been rounded for convenience.

LIQUID/DRY MEASUREMENTS	
U.S.	**Metric**
¼ teaspoon	1.25 milliliters
½ teaspoon	2.5 milliliters
1 teaspoon	5 milliliters
1 tablespoon (3 teaspoons)	15 milliliters
1 fluid ounce (2 tablespoons)	30 milliliters
¼ cup	60 milliliters
⅓ cup	80 milliliters
½ cup	120 milliliters
1 cup	240 milliliters

LIQUID/DRY MEASUREMENTS	
U.S.	**Metric**
1 pint (2 cups)	480 milliliters
1 quart (4 cups; 32 ounces)	960 milliliters
1 gallon (4 quarts)	3.84 liters
1 ounce (by weight)	28 grams
1 pound	448 grams
2.2 pounds	1 kilogram

LENGTHS	
U.S.	**Metric**
⅛ inch	3 millimeters
¼ inch	6 millimeters
½ inch	12 millimeters
1 inch	2.5 centimeters

OVEN TEMPERATURES		
Fahrenheit	**Celsius**	**Gas**
250	120	½
275	140	1
300	150	2
325	160	3
350	180	4
375	190	5
400	200	6
425	220	7
450	230	8
475	240	9
500	260	10